MW00614880

Female Pioneers of Fort Myers

Women Who Made a Difference in the City's Development

Robin C. Tuthill
Thomas P. Hall

Published by Editorial Rx Press
Editorial Rx Press, Registered Office:
3233 Eleanor Way, North Fort Myers, FL 33917
www.editorialrxpress.com

First Editorial Rx Press Printing, November 2015

10 9 8 7 6 5 4 3 2 1

ISBN 978-0-9832958-3-9

Printed in the United States of America.

Original cover and book design by Biographics
www.biographicsweb.com

Front cover: Mina Miller Edison (bottom left, courtesy of Edison & Ford Winter Estates); Evalina Gonzalez (bottom right, courtesy of Southwest Florida Museum of History); Flossie Hill (center, courtesy of Southwest Florida Museum of History); Tootie McGregor Terry (top left, courtesy of Southwest Florida Historical Society); Ella Mae Piper (top right, courtesy of Lee County Black History Society).

Back cover: Florida Schultz Heitman (courtesy of Southwest Florida Historical Society), Veronica Shoemaker (courtesy of Lee County Black History Society), Laura Jane Hendry Thompson (courtesy of Southwest Florida Historical Society) (left to right, top row); Olive Stout (bottom row, courtesy of Southwest Florida Historical Society).

DEDICATION

Robin

To my mother, Dorothy Jean Frakes Tuthill (1923-1984), who taught me to play Anagrams when I was 6, who loved fishing all day and camping out near the mangroves at night, and who would be so happy that her daughter got to bring these strong, Florida pioneer women's stories into the present.

And to Linda J. Allen, whose support for the last 20 years has given me the time and space to pursue my love of reading, writing, and empowering others to find healing, happiness, and self-transformation through writing their stories.

Words are a form of action, capable of influencing change.
—Ingrid Bengis, American writer

Tom

To the love of my life, Connie Keller, who exemplifies the qualities and attributes of the strong, determined and other-directed women whose stories we share in the pages that follow.

Contents

ACKNOWLEDGMENTS

Many of the women featured in this book partnered with each other, creating positive coalitions to actualize their vision for what Fort Myers could and should be. In the same vein, we have reached out to a number of people for their insight, input and technical support in connection with this project. We would like to recognize their contributions here, starting with Southwest Florida Museum of History Research Director Jim Powers for his thorough reading of our manuscript with a keen eye for detail and finely honed sense of historical context. Many thanks also to the Southwest Florida Historical Society. Their volunteer staff provided friendly and helpful assistance in locating the last three images we needed.

Gerri Reaves is known to many in Southwest Florida as *The River Weekly News'* history columnist and as author of *Legendary Locals of Fort Myers and Fort Myers, Then & Now.* As busy as she is, Gerri generously took the time to read our entire manuscript, not only fact-checking the contents but ensuring we got the town's irregular geography and quirky lay-out exactly right.

We are also grateful to Theresa M. Schober for her encouragement and endorsement. An archaeologist and anthropologist, Theresa has worked assiduously to uncover the early history of Southwest Florida, focusing on the native Calusa and early Spanish settlers starting with Ponce de Leon and Pedro Menendez de Aviles. In addition to directing restoration of the historic Mound House on Fort Myers Beach, she coordinated the two-year Lee Trust for Historic Preservation and Florida Humanities Council project, Making History Memorable, and is completing work on a documentary film about Mound Key, which served as the capitol of the mighty Calusa nation for hundreds of years.

We are very appreciative of Edison & Ford Winter Estates President Chris Pendleton and Chief Curator Mike Cosden. They did not just read our manuscript to verify its accuracy with respect to our account of the contributions made to Fort Myers' development by Mina Edison and Helen Hendry. They studied the text, noted where it could be enriched by the addition of a few details known to them but few others, and then met with us in person to supply the details and background necessary to appreciate their significance.

We extend great thanks to author Doris Weatherford, whose publications include *They Dared to Dream: Florida Women Who Shaped History* (2015),

Women and American Politics: History and Milestones (which won an American Library Association award), *History of the American Suffragist Movement*, and numerous other volumes involving women in history and politics. Doris went the extra mile while reading the manuscript and provided an important correction in the spelling of the "Fort Myers Woman's Club."

We also appreciate the help and, more, the ardor that the Lee County Black History Society voiced for this project. No account of the contributions made by our female pioneers would be complete without inclusion of those made by Dr. Ella Mae Piper, Melissa Jones, Candis Walker and Veronica Shoemaker. They supplied us with rare facts and even rarer photographs of these important personages, whose reach extended far beyond the Dunbar community (known back then as Safety Hill).

The *Fort Myers News-Press* generously shared valuable historical photographs from their archives, which accounts for many key photos included here. We are grateful to local artists Linda Busch Benson, Cindy Jane and Africa Valdez for permitting us to use images of the portraits they rendered of Veronica Shoemaker, Ella Mae Piper and Olive Stout for the Fort Myers Founding Females portrait show that hung in the historic Caretaker's Cottage at the Edison Ford Estates from December of 2014 through May of 2015. Nearly 200,000 people had the opportunity to take in that show, and the interest and enthusiasm they evinced factored into our decision to craft written portraits of the women who helped settle Fort Myers and transform it from an unrefined frontier town into a sophisticated cultural and tourist center.

We wish to express our appreciation for the interest that Mayor Randy Henderson has taken in our project. Mayor Henderson has always exercised great responsibility for promoting the city's rich and fabled heritage, and he is an enthusiastic advocate for our efforts to both expand and balance Fort Myers' legacy by including accounts of the women who did their own part to create and publicize our town's amenities and advantages to the world beyond.

Finally, this book would not have come to life without the patience, expertise and commitment of our publisher Deb Whippen, of Editorial Rx Press, Inc. In a fortunate stroke of serendipity, Deb encountered Robin and Tom's project after the successful publication of *Memoirs of an Everglades Pioneer,* which launched a new line of Southwest Florida regional books. We look forward to a working partnership for a long time to come, as this book has spurred ideas for several related projects.

FOREWORD

By Amy Bennett Williams

They wrestled tarpon, started hospitals and bred hibiscus. Shopkeepers and beauticians, socialites and teachers, the women celebrated in *Female Pioneers of Fort Myers: Women Who Made a Difference in the City's Development* may have had wildly different lives and times, but each helped forge this vibrant subtropical city.

Some of their names are familiar to residents, who pass them daily on street signs or cultural centers. Others will likely be new to readers, no matter how versed they are in area history. One of the distinct pleasures of this book is discovering the ways this diverse corps of women contributed to the City of Palms. Authors Robin C. Tuthill and Thomas P. Hall sketch vivid biographies of more than 20 trailblazing women who left their mark on Fort Myers, weaving together a portrait of female achievement that completes the often male-centrically lopsided versions of the region's history.

One of the media's most important duties is to make the past real—and riveting—for contemporary consumers. In the nearly three decades I've written for the *Fort Myers News-Press*, I've tried to contribute to that effort, and along the way, I've had the honor of knowing several of the women highlighted in these pages, and the pleasure of researching others. To have them gathered in one place as they are here is a gift to any student of the past and to generations to come.

Some of the women included in the book rubbed shoulders—or hands— during their fascinating lifetimes. Take, for example, Mina Edison and Ella Piper. One was the wife of a celebrity inventor, the other a self-made entrepreneur in an age when most women, let alone black women, couldn't dream of building their own thriving businesses. Yet Ella parlayed her success as a chiropodist (her clients included Mina), into success as a bottling company owner and philanthropist. The two stood side-by-side at the 1937 dedication of Dunbar High School, which Ella helped spearhead and Mina helped landscape. One of Mina's husband's famous rubber trees still shades the gracious building. Both women's generosity in death continues to enrich Fort Myers: Mina deeded her home and grounds to the city, as did Ella, for "the benefit of the children, the poor and the elderly in the black community."

Some of the featured woman never met, but are nonetheless kindred spirits. I've long thought, for example, that Tootie McGregor and Berne Davis would have been great friends. Though Berne was born two years after Tootie died, each made huge contributions to the city they both adopted as home. Never mind their divergent backgrounds—Tootie was the well-off daughter of an Ohio judge, while Berne grew up wringing chicken's necks in lumber camps—the two manifested landscape-changing love for Fort Myers. We have Tootie to thank for the city's iconic McGregor Boulevard, and it was Berne's gift that helped make reality the downtown art center that bears her name, along with her late husband, Sidney's. Both women knew deep love and loss, as the book shows, and they shared a gently self-deprecating estimation of their own impact.

Berne routinely waves away praise for her philanthropy, implying that what she does is simply what anyone else would. And Tootie once wrote, "I only hope the little I have done may be an incentive to others to do more" - words her husband had inscribed on the memorial fountain that now graces the Fort Myers Country Club.

With all due respect, I must disagree.

"Little" is hardly the word to describe what Tootie and the others honored in these pages contributed.

Indeed, we're indebted to these women for many of the cultural institutions we hold dearest, and in this groundbreaking book, Tuthill and Hall show just how crucial their gifts, their labor and their lives have been to the city they all shaped.

Amy Bennett Williams
The News-Press *senior writer and author of "Along the Caloosahatchee River"*
Alva, Florida

INTRODUCTION

Present-day Fort Myers is the product of tough, courageous, strong-willed pioneers who built a rough-and-tumble cow town out of the remnants of an abandoned frontier fort in the years following the end of the Civil War. But the town's early historians only chronicled the contributions made by the charismatic, often idiosyncratic cattlemen, shopkeepers, land developers, and entrepreneurs who transformed the settlement (where cows and hogs freely roamed, ravaged and defiled the streets) into a center for citrus packing and tourism.

Women made significant contributions as well. But for those of Christiana Vivas and Jane L. Hendry, there would in all likelihood be no Fort Myers today. For myriad reasons, the names and accomplishments of these female visionaries were largely relegated to footnotes or parentheticals in the annals that recounted the achievements of their male counterparts.

An important part of our heritage is lost when any segment of the population is denied recognition and credit for the important strides it makes in enriching the lives of the community and contributing to its legacy in the arts, business, education and civic leadership. With this thought in mind, *Female Pioneers of Fort Myers* brings the personal stories of 24 remarkable women to the forefront so that current and future generations of Southwest Florida residents and visitors can learn and benefit from their examples of self-sacrifice, refusal to conform to the social norms of their day, and the self-confidence to manifest their unique vision for the future.

The book operates on two levels. On an individual level, it shares for the very first time the rich personal stories of a group of exceptional women who suffered and overcame rigorous hardships, incomprehensible loss and numbing tragedies to create dynamic legacies. On a broader plane, their collective contributions and impact on their contemporaries and future generations demonstrate that anyone is capable of great things, regardless of gender, race, or any other personal attribute that falls outside the culturally perceived "norm."

From that perspective, *Female Pioneers of Fort Myers* is not just for readers who have an interest in local history. Rather, it offers education and inspiration for us all. In particular, we believe the stories of these ordinary women who did extraordinary things will provide positive female role models for both girls and boys at a time when examples like these are conspicuously absent in traditional media outlets, including film, television, and even video games. After all, what better role models are there for the young women and men living and going to school here in Southwest Florida than the real-life women from our collective past who were actually responsible for settling and developing our town?

Reporting in a reader-friendly, conversational tone that has never before been presented, the first section of *Female Pioneers of Fort Myers* portrays 13 women who significantly impacted the development of the town's culture, buildings and amenities from 1866 through the early 1900s. But women achieved many "firsts," and the second part of our book, titled "More Notable Women," includes the charming stories of Fort Myers' first daughter, the woman for whom the old fort was named, the town's first school teacher, and some important civic leaders and philanthropists like Veronica Shoemaker and Berne Davis, who made more recent life-changing contributions to the fabric of our community and culture.

Whether you just want to be entertained by stories of heroic women who lived in another epoch, or be inspired by an iconoclastic group of gritty pioneer women, you will find it here in *Female Pioneers of Fort Myers*.

Enjoy!

TIMELINE

1850   On Valentine's Day, Major General David Emmanuel Twiggs sends two companies of soldiers to establish an outpost "deep in Seminole Indian territory." As a gift to his daughter, Marion Isabelle Twiggs, he names the post Fort Myers to honor her fiancé, Colonel Abraham C. Myers, who had served admirably under Twiggs' command.

1857   Ada Elizabeth Hancock is the first non-Native American baby born in Fort Myers.

1861-
1865   Civil War

1866   Manual Gonzalez becomes first permanent settler of Fort Myers; three weeks later Joseph and Christiana Vivas arrive and stake a claim. Christiana is the first female settler.

Evalina Weatherford Gonzalez becomes first schoolteacher, homeschooling four children.

1872   Surveyors announce that homesteading up to 160 acres of land will soon be possible. Everybody moves out of town to homestead, except for Joseph and Christiana Vivas.

1873   Jane L. Hendry—the "Mother" of Fort Myers—moves family into town, likely saving the town from becoming deserted.

Laura Jane Hendry, daughter of F.A. and Ardeline Hendry, marries Waddy Thompson, making Laura the first bride of Fort Myers.

1876   Establishment of a post office.

1879   Mary Verdier Parker is Fort Myers' first paid female schoolteacher.

1882   Sarah Kantz Knight Titus and her brother Daniel Kantz move to Fort Myers and build the town's first hotel, The Keystone.

1884   First issue of *Fort Myers Press* by former New York newspaper publisher Stafford Cleveland.

British born Julia Allen Hanson settles in Fort Myers when she and her physician husband discover the "tiny cow town" on their way to Cuba. So influential, she becomes known as "Most Beloved Woman in Florida" and "Mother of all Women's Clubs."

1885   Fort Myers incorporated, population 349.

First tarpon ever caught with a rod and reel boated off Punta Rassa. The 93-pound silver king that took W.H. Wood 26-1/2 minutes to land generated illustrated articles in many of the leading magazines of the day and put Fort Myers on the map as the tarpon capital of the world. (Prior to this, tarpon had always been caught using a shark hook and chain line or by harpooning them.)

1886   Olive and Frank Stout move to Fort Myers from Central Florida to buy the 15-month old *Fort Myers Press*. Olive remains affiliated with the newspaper for the next 27 years.

Mina Miller Edison arrives in Fort Myers as Thomas Edison's bride, and over the next 60 years makes invaluable contributions and improvements to the community.

Thomas Edison builds winter home–"Seminole Lodge."

1887   Lee County created.

1889   Olive Stout appointed postmaster by President William McKinley. Re-appointed to the position in 1897 by President Teddy Roosevelt.

1892   Tootie and Ambrose McGregor establish a winter home in Fort Myers.

1895   Candis Walker (later of Jones-Walker Hospital fame), one of the nine founders of the Fort Myers Mount Olive A.M.E. Church, attends first organizational meeting for the church, held in the Lee County Courthouse.

1897   Fort Myers' first brick building at the northwest corner of First and Jackson, built by Harvie Heitman and financed by Ambrose McGregor.

Florida Abbie Schultz marries Harvie Heitman.

1898   Fort Myers becomes a nationally known winter resort destination with the building of the Royal Palm Hotel.

1900   Alice Hendry Tooke McCann, daughter of Jane L. and Charles Hendry, becomes the town's first telephone switchboard operator.

Olive Stout partners with Flossie Hill, Florida Heitman and Julia Hanson to form the Fort Myers Woman's Club.

Population of Fort Myers is 943.

1903   Flossie Hill leads a group of women in fighting the Great Fire and saves the town from certain destruction.

Created by the Fort Myers Woman's Club, a public reading room opens; closes in late 1904 when land clearing begins for the Bradford Hotel; re-opens in another location in February 1906. Olive Stout serves as first librarian.

by 1904   Fort Myers has electric lights, telephone system, fire department, and railroad station.

1904   Tootie McGregor and Harvie Heitman team up to build the Bradford Hotel, which opens in 1905.

Julia Isabel Frierson Hendry, a former Miss Tampa, drives the last spike in the railroad ties that brought the Atlantic Coast Line Railroad to Fort Myers.

1905   Tootie McGregor marries her high school sweetheart, Dr. Marshall Terry.

Flossie Hill opens Fort Myers' first department store, the M. Flossie Hill Department Store, also known as the Ladies Trading Place.

Mary Laycock, dedicated to keeping the reading room running, chairs the Funds Solicitation Committee 1905-1926, when the reading room culminated in the Fort Myers Library.

1906   Tootie and Marshall Terry donate 40 acres to the newly formed Fort Myers Yacht and Country Club in an effort to bring golf to the town. The land was converted in 1926 into a spring training facility for the Philadelphia Athletics.

1907   Tootie McGregor purchases the Royal Palm and campaigns to change riverscape, resulting in construction of a seawall along the riverfront that eventually extended from Monroe all the way to Billy's Creek.

Florida Schultz Heitman bands together with nine other women to form a civic league to clean up and beautify the town.

1912   Tootie McGregor convinces city to pave Riverside from Whiskey Creek to downtown Fort Myers, in exchange for Tootie paving the 20-mile stretch from Whiskey Creek to Punta Rassa. She also set up a fund to maintain the road for the next five years, but she died before construction began. The name of the newly paved road was changed to McGregor Boulevard in honor of her first husband.

1913   To memorialize all that his wife had done to further the town's development, Marshall Terry installs the Tootie McGregor Fountain, Fort Myers' first public art piece.

1916   Ella Mae Piper opens the town's first beauty salon. In addition to haircare, Ella provides chiropody, or foot care, now commonly called podiatry.

1920   19th Amendment to the U.S. Constitution grants American women the right to vote. (The women's suffrage movement had been waged state-by-state and many Western states had already granted women the right to vote, led by Wyoming in 1869.)

1923   10-year-old Barbara Balch (later, Mann) moves to Fort Myers with her mother and sister. A talented pianist and singer, Barbara B. Mann becomes a veritable champion of the arts and is instrumental in the founding of almost every arts organization in the county.

1924   Melissa Jones and Candis Walker spearhead effort to raise monies to build the first hospital to serve the black community of Lee County. Prior to this, seriously ill patients were transported to Tampa or Key West for hospitalization, as black patients were not allowed at Lee Memorial. The dedication of the Jones-Walker Hospital in the Dunbar community was in 1924, but it had to be rebuilt two years later after the Hurricane of 1926 destroyed the first building.

1926   (ca.) Ella Mae Piper petitions the state for permission to buy and sell property and conduct business independently. Even though in the 1920s married women were not allowed to own or manage their own businesses without their husbands' approval, the state grants Ella's request.

When Sarah Williams, Ella Mae Piper's mother, dies, Ella takes over the annual Christmas party that Sarah had started in 1915 at her home in Safety Hill, now called Dunbar. Still a Dunbar tradition, the Christmas party celebrates its centennial in December 2015.

1927   Florida Schultz Heitman helps to form the Caloosahatchee Chapter of the Daughters of the American Revolution and maintains an active membership until 1945.

1937   Ella Mae Piper, with Mina Edison on stage beside her, helps to dedicate the city's first public black high school, Dunbar High. At that time mixing of the races was usually unacceptable and Mina had to be privately escorted in to the event as a special guest.

1940s   Veronica Shoemaker begins to establish herself as a community leader and spokesperson while a student at Dunbar High School.

1942   Helen Johnson (Hendry), at age 12, begins working at Everglades Nursery, the first nursery in South Florida, setting the stage for a trailblazing career in horticulture and landscape architecture. She becomes the first female certified by the State of Florida's Board of Landscape Architects.

1969   Lee County school system is fully desegregated, 15 years after the U.S. Supreme Court ruling mandating school desegregation and five years after passage of the Civil Rights Act of 1964.

1982   Veronica Shoemaker is the first African American to serve on the Fort Myers City Council, a position she held for 26 years, elected after 17 years of campaigning for public office.

2005   Berne Davis donates $1 million to kick off the drive to raise the $6 million needed for restoration and rehabilitation of the old post office. The Sidney & Berne Davis Art Center not only revitalized the downtown area but will influence generations to come of new visual and performing artists, filmmakers and educators.

2009   Berne Davis named by the Southwest Florida Museum of History Foundation as the first recipient of its History Maker of the Year Award.

1864 Map of Florida
(Johnson & Ward Atlas)

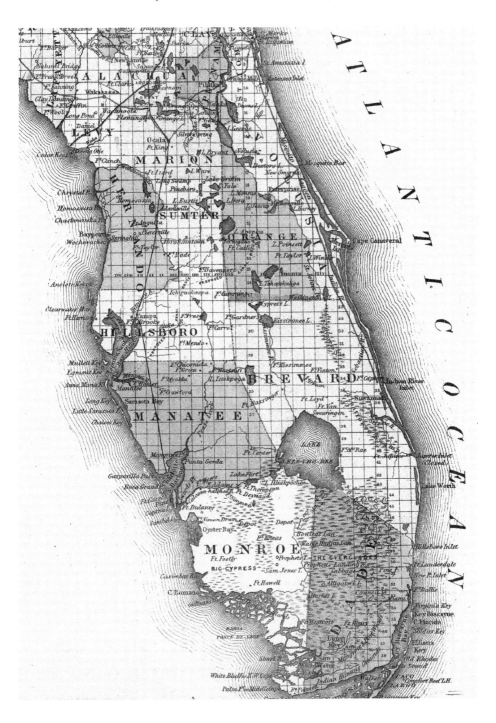

Profiles of
Female Pioneers

CHRISTIANA STIRRUP VIVAS

Fort Myers' First Female Settler

Fort Myers' first female settler was a child the first time she laid eyes on the frontier outpost that sprawled along the south shore of the broad, slow-flowing Caloosahatchee River. It had been built beginning in 1850 to round up and deport the last of the Seminoles to Indian Territory in Oklahoma. Christiana's dad was Manuel Gonzalez, who captained a schooner that brought mail, commissary and other supplies to the soldiers stationed at the fort. He often brought his wife, Evalina, on these runs, and on one trip he also brought Christiana, an orphan of English descent that the couple was raising as their own.

One can only imagine how the fort must have appeared to an impressionable girl of just six or seven. She saw a compound of 57 buildings–barracks, kitchens, laundry facilities, as well as officers' quarters, a wagon yard and stables, blacksmith and carpentry shops, a bakery and a hospital. The post even boasted a bathing pier and pavilion, bowling alley, and two immense vegetable gardens.

"The fort presented a beautiful appearance," wrote F.A. Hendry following a memorable visit to the post in 1854. "The grounds were tastefully laid out with shell walks and dress parade grounds and beautifully adorned with many kinds of palms. The velvety lawn was carefully tended. Special care was given to the rock-rimmed river banks. The long lines of uniformed soldiers with white gloves and burnished guns, and the officers with their golden epaulettes and shining side arms were grand and magnificent to behold. The officers and men were very courteous and kind, and a more comfortable set of men I never saw."

Still the "finest spot in the entire state for building a home"

But that beauty did not last. During the final year of the Civil War, Fort Myers had been manned by Union soldiers. They used the old Seminole Indian war post as a base of operations from which to raid cattle from ranchers located up the west coast of the peninsula. When the war ended, former Confederate soldiers from as far away as Manatee, Pinellas and Cedar Key sailed down the coast in sloops and schooners. Here they found wood and building materials they desperately needed to repair and rebuild the homes they had neglected during the war. They ripped up flooring, tore windows and doors from their frames, pried loose siding and cedar shingles from the roofs, and carried it all away.

During his repeated trips between Key West and Tampa in the 1850s, Gonzalez had become intimately familiar with Southwest Florida and was convinced that Fort Myers was the finest spot in the entire state for building a home. He returned on February 21, 1866, to do just that, but must have been shocked at the sight of the picked-over remnants of the once-proud fort. In spite of the fort's ramshackle condition, he decided to stay and make his home out of the remains of the former eight-room commanding officers' quarters. Gonzalez, his five-year-old son Manuel, his brother-in-law, John Weatherford, and old family friend Joe Vivas pitched their tents on the hospital grounds.

Christiana Stirrup Vivas in 1930, in front of her riverfront homestead. (Courtesy of Southwest Florida Historical Society.)

Gonzalez must have felt secure in planning to build here because so little remained of the once magnificent facility that there was little danger of someone coming in and buying the fort property from the federal government. So Gonzalez sent Weatherford and Vivas back to Key West for Evalina, the kids, and their belongings while he remained behind with little Manuel and began piecing the officers' quarters back into a fully functioning home.

There is no record of when or how Christiana and Joe's feelings for each other had come about, but they wed in Key West on March 8, shortly after Joe's return. Then 21-year-old Joe and his 16-year-old bride boarded Joe's sailboat and set sail for Fort Myers. That's where Christiana found her dad and brother, adding the finishing touches to the Gonzalez's new home.

From girl to frontier woman
An excellent carpenter, Joe immediately rebuilt a small log cabin just east of the Gonzalez home. Joe and Manuel replanted the gardens that the soldiers had once maintained with sweet potatoes, melons, pumpkins and vegetables. Bilingual, they earned income by serving as interpreters for Spanish brokers who came from Cuba to Punta Rassa to buy cattle from F.A. Hendry and Cracker King Jake Summerlin.

While life in the picturesque two-family community was unquestionably hard—after all, they had broken ground in a veritable wilderness teeming with snakes, alligators, panthers, and biting insects—the climate was temperate, fishing abundant, and the soil fertile. Fort Myers became home to new wife and mother Christiana, and two more settlers joined the Gonzalez-Weatherford-

Some of the first riverfront homesteads. The two-story house that Joe Vivas built in 1883 is pictured toward the back of this 1886 sketch. (Courtesy of Southwest Florida Historical Society.)

Vivas clan the next year. One was a citrus grower by the name of John Powell. The other was moonshiner Bill Clay.* Fort Myers' first black settler, farmer and fishing guide Nelson Tillis, arrived in 1867 on the same boat as Powell and Clay, but settled his large family a little further north of the riverfront.

Evalina Gonzalez set up shop as the town's first schoolteacher, home-schooling her own and the Powells' two children. Manuel opened a small general store behind his refurbished home, trading with a handful of Seminoles who lived in Big Cypress swamp and cattle drovers passing through town with herds of scrub cows bound for Punta Rassa and Key West, Havana and beyond. But business was far from brisk, so when a survey party arrived in February 1872 with news that it would soon be possible to homestead up to 160 acres of land, everyone abandoned Fort Myers except Christiana and Joe.

By the spring of 1872, Christiana clearly had strong emotional ties to the town. Not only did the fort occupy a heartfelt place among her fondest childhood memories, the little log cabin that Joe built was where they had honeymooned, where she had borne her first child and where she'd changed from a girl into a frontier woman. So rather than follow the rest of their small community and move, Christiana and Joe remained behind, preventing the tiny town from being completely abandoned and setting the foundation for Jane L. Hendry's decision a year later to move her family to Fort Myers. F.A. Hendry followed Jane and her husband, Charles, as did his brother, Marion, his sister, Mary Jane Blount, and two nephews. This group along with the Vivases built the nearly deserted town into a thriving rough-and-tumble cow town in the last third of the 19th century.

Christiana and Joe lived in their cozy log cabin until 1883. In that year, Joe replaced it with a fine two-story house which he built from material he had shipped in from Cedar Key. Joe died in 1909, survived by Christiana and their nine children.

Christiana died in 1930, at the age of 79. While she will always hold the honor of being Fort Myers' first female settler and honeymooner, the town owes its very existence to Christiana Stirrup Vivas. Had she and Joe deserted Fort Myers in 1872 along with everyone else, there would have been no neigh-bors to attract Jane and Charles Hendry a year later, depriving them and the rest of the Hendry clan of their primary motivation to move into town.

----

*Bill Clay became one of the region's most notorious moonshiners. He operated a still on a creek—"Whiskey Creek"—that was on a route that cowboys and Seminole Indians used.

EVALINA WEATHERFORD GONZALEZ

Fort Myers' First Schoolteacher

Evalina Weatherford Gonzalez holds the distinction of being Fort Myers first schoolteacher, but she also had a hand in the decision to settle the town in the months following the end of the Civil War. Evalina was born in the Bahamas in 1836. While in Key West, she met and married Manuel A. Gonzalez. Originally from Madrid, Manuel had sailed for Cuba at the age of 14 with a group of other boys. The trip almost proved disastrous as the ship wrecked in a storm on the east coast of Florida. All on board managed to swim ashore and a few years later Manuel made his way to Key West, where he became a U.S. citizen.

From Key West to Fort Myers
In spite of his near death experience on his maiden voyage to the New World, Manuel became a sea captain. During the Third Seminole War, he delivered mail and supplies between Tampa and Key West. One of his stops was a post on the Caloosahatchee River known as Fort Myers.

Evalina accompanied Manuel on many of these trips and the couple fell in love with the area around the fort so much that they decided to one day make it their home. That day came in February 1866 when Manuel set sail for the old fort along with his 5-year-old son, brother-in-law John Weatherford, and their close family friend, Joe Vivas.

Although the fort had been cannibalized by Confederate soldiers returning to their homes in Tampa and Cedar Key from the Civil War, Manuel decided to stay, and dispatched John Weatherford and Joe Vivas for Key West to get Evalina, the children and their things. Evalina joined him a few weeks later. By then, father and son had pieced together the commanding officer's quarters into a fine two-story, eight-room house that would stand for another seven decades. Manuel even built a general store behind the house that catered to nearby Seminoles and drovers passing by the fort with herds of scrub cows bound for the shipping pens at Punta Rassa. Running the store was more of a side income, and in the years after they relocated to the Caloosahatchee, Manuel continued to make a living as a seaman. He also served as an interpreter for the wealthy cattle brokers who came from Cuba to buy steers.

Children's education will not be neglected
In all likelihood, Evalina staffed the general store during her husband's absences, but she also most likely supplemented the family's earnings by schooling the neighbor's children. Those neighbors were John Powell and Bill Clay, who came to the settlement a year after the Gonzalezes. "The mother of a large family, Mrs. Gonzalez was determined that the education of her children should not be neglected even though they were living at the end of nowhere," writes historian Karl Grismer in his 1948 book, *The Story of Fort Myers*. "Her husband brought in textbooks from Key West and Mrs. Gonzalez started holding classes in her home in the fall of 1868."

No other families joined the small settlement in the next five years. So when a survey crew arrived in February 1872, announcing that it would soon

Evalina Weatherford Gonzalez was determined that her children's education would not be neglected even though they were living "at the end of nowhere." (Courtesy of Southwest Florida Museum of History.)

Manuel A. Gonzalez. (Courtesy of Southwest Florida Historical Society.)

be possible for them to homestead up to 160 acres of land, Manuel and Evalina decided to move out of town to a spread of land west of the old fort that had a clear creek running through it. The rest of the neighborhood followed suit, except for Joe and Christiana Vivas. The decision to move must have been difficult for Evalina as she and Manuel had raised Christiana, who had been orphaned when she was a very young girl.

Evalina and Manuel lived on the homestead for nearly 20 years, but they moved back into town in the 1890s. They built a residence on Monroe Street, which Evalina later sold for $6,000 to the Atlantic Coast Line Railroad. By then, Manuel had died, and Evalina had relocated a few blocks away to a beautiful three-story Victorian home that still exists today.

The home was one of two that Evalina's son, Manuel S. Gonzalez (then 41), built on the corner of Broadway and Second Street. He and his family occupied the corner house, and Evalina moved into the other. The two houses were joined together in the early 1970s by Peter Pulitzer, son of the publisher, with the original kitchen building from the mother's house, along with a secluded garden courtyard, joining the two houses together. The co-joined home was purchased in 1978 by Paul Peden and transformed into The Veranda, one of the River District's pre-eminent downtown restaurants.

While Evalina Weatherford Gonzalez will forever hold the distinction of being Fort Myers' first schoolteacher, albeit private, it is clear from the historical record that she played a pivotal role in the decision to make Fort Myers the Gonzalez's home. She remained loyal to the town and resided there until her death in 1933.

In 1866 Manuel Gonzalez built the two-story, eight-room house, pictured on the right, that would stand for another seven decades. (Courtesy of Southwest Florida Museum of History.)

Jane L. Hendry

"Mother" of Fort Myers

On a May morning in 1873, Jane Louise Hendry (née Brown) awoke to find her 6-year-old daughter, Esther Ann, moaning with a high fever. Jane, her husband, Charles, and their four children lived in a two-room shack in pastureland some 30 miles east of the old fort in present-day Immokalee. But Charles was out on the range and had not been home in three days, and Jane had no one to help her care for the stricken child.

Jane flagged down a passing Indian, who came running. "Bad sick," he said when he laid eyes on little Esther Ann. "Soon go to big sleep." Somehow Jane made the Seminole understand that she needed her husband, and he took off to track down the cattleman. Charles galloped home that afternoon. Esther Ann died that night.

Burying a child

As soon as Esther Ann's crude wood coffin was lowered into the grave that Charles and his cousins dug the following morning beneath a pine tree, Jane went inside and began packing. When Charles asked her what she was doing, she spun around on the heel of one boot and let him know in no uncertain terms that she had no intention of spending another night in the wilderness far from neighbors. She would be near help the next time one of her children fell ill. She was joining Joe and Christiana Vivas in Fort Myers. Charles knew she was right. He had always had misgivings about moving his family so far out in Glades country just so he could keep his eye on the Hendrys' herds. So he helped Jane pack. His cousins, F.A., Marion and Abner Hendry also lent a hand. It didn't take long. Pioneer homes were not lavishly appointed. All their furniture and other belongings fit on just two oxcarts.

It took Jane, Charles and their three remaining children four days to make the trip. There were no roads leading into town from that direction, so they had to forge a trail through the sand, palmetto and scrub pines. They moved into a small log cabin with a thatched roof at the edge of Billy's Creek that had once served as a shelter for sentries during the Third Seminole War. (After the hurricane of October 6, 1873, the Hendrys would move to the fort site itself, acquiring the place just east of present-day Monroe that moonshiner Bill Clay had vacated the year before.)

Following Jane's lead, F.A. Hendry and Marion Hendry, Charles' cousins, moved their families to Fort Myers that June. F.A. rebuilt one of the former officers' quarters just east of the Vivas' cabin near present-day First Street and Royal Palm Boulevard. Marion rebuilt an old building on the river bank just east of the fort's 750-foot pier, which was located at the foot of present-day Hendry Street. Three more families, all related to the Hendrys, soon followed.

Settling in Fort Myers

The Hendrys were very familiar with the old fort. They had often passed through its grounds on cattle drives downriver to Punta Rassa. F.A. had

Jane L. Hendry in front of the home she built on First Street. From left to right, granddaughter Amazon "Ammie" Tooke, daughter Alice McCann, granddaughter Josephine, Claudia Baxter Stroup, and (far right) Jane. (Courtesy of Southwest Florida Historical Society.)

1889 photo of First Street. (Courtesy of Southwest Florida Museum of History.)

visited the fort twice during the Third Seminole War, first as a dispatch bearer in 1854 and a year later as a guide for a cavalry company in which he later enlisted and became a lieutenant. F.A. also captained a company of soldiers in the Cattle Guard Battalion when Confederate Colonel J. Munnerlyn attacked the fort on February 20, 1865 in a skirmish that has come to be known as The Battle of Fort Myers. Marion had been an officer in the Cattle Guard Battalion too, and Charles had taken Seminole prisoners to the fort in the 1850s while a member of the Florida Volunteers boat company.

Although Jane and Charles and their relatives joined Joe and Christiana Vivas as settlers, they were, in reality, squatters. What they did not know was that while they were busy building houses and making Fort Myers their home, a former surveyor from Virginia named James Evans had homesteaded the 139.45 acres in and surrounding the fort. Evans had been part of a survey party that had visited the abandoned fort in 1859. He had liked the area so much that he'd stayed behind when the rest of the surveyors moved on. Intending to homestead the land one day, he planted hundreds of coconut palms, an acre of tropical plants and bushes, and even some coffee plants he obtained in Key West. But when the Civil War started, he returned to Virginia and joined the Confederate Army. Now, he was filing the paperwork necessary to finalize his claim.

Evans could have legally ousted everyone from his land, but he wisely chose to sell the settlers the property on which they'd built their homes. While theories abound to explain why Evans did this, it is clear that the remaining

On the Wells Fargo Home Mortgage bank building next door to Val Ward Cadillac in Fort Myers is a mosaic attributed to Millard Sheets. It is one of more than 175 stained glass, mosaics and painted murals that Sheets' studio created. Sheets' studio always featured some important scene from the community's local history in its mosaics and murals. Although the inscription beneath the Fort Myers' mosaic reads "McGregor Boulevard, once a cattle trail, is today lined by stately palms. The pride of Fort Myers. Among the boulevard founders: Thomas Edison, James E. Hendry, Jr., Tootie McGregor Terry, Ambrose McGregor," the scene actually depicted looks very much like Charles and Jane L. Hendry's oxcart exodus from Glades country to Fort Myers in May of 1873, complete with a resolute woman leading a paint horse bearing two young children. (Courtesy of Thomas P. Hall, Art Southwest Florida.)

property had more value as part of a thriving settlement, and it made more sense to have the Hendrys as allies than enemies.

Fort Myers' first female real estate owner/dealer

For just $1, Jane purchased most of the waterfront between present-day Monroe and Hendry and all the way back to Second Street, making her the town's first female real estate owner. She became Fort Myers' first female real estate dealer several years later when newly formed Lee County came calling, looking for a site on which to build a courthouse. She made a handsome profit, selling the two-acre tract bounded by Main, Broadway, Second and Monroe in September 1889 for the sum of $2,250.

Jane did leave Fort Myers for a period of time. Beginning in 1883, Charles began spending more and more time in Key West, where he brokered the cattle shipped in by the Hendrys and Dr. T.E. Langford. Key West was a five-day trip from Fort Myers in those days, so Jane and the children soon joined Charles, and they lived there until Charles' death in 1893. After laying her husband to rest, Jane moved back to Fort Myers, building a home on the corner of First and Broadway, on the site of what is now the Franklin Shops. She lived there until her death in 1908.

In the years from Jane's return to Fort Myers until her death, the town became a bustling cow town due in large measure to F.A. Hendry's cattle business. Between 1873 and his retirement in 1888, F.A. built a herd of more than 50,000 head. His operation attracted scores of cow hunters, drovers, blacksmiths, cobblers, shopkeepers, doctors and druggists from all over Florida. In addition to being the town's largest and most affluent employer, F.A. took an active role in nearly every civic and political decision affecting the community. He was appointed Chairman of the committee that voted to incorporate the town in1885. He was one of the town's seminal city councilmen. And it was F.A. who recommended that the county be named in honor of Robert E. Lee when the area broke away from Monroe County in 1887.

Not surprisingly, Francis Asbury Hendry—"F.A."—became known as the "Father" of Fort Myers and is credited today with founding the town that grew out of the debris of the old Seminole Indian and Civil War fort. However, had Jane not decided to move to Fort Myers after the death of little Esther Ann, it is unlikely that either F.A. or Marion Hendry would have moved there. In fact, but for the death of the six-year-old girl and her mother's emphatic decision to move near neighbors, Fort Myers may very well have been deserted. It could certainly be argued that that decision should make Jane L. Hendry the "Mother" of Fort Myers.

LAURA JANE HENDRY THOMPSON

Fort Myers' First Bride

While Laura Jane Hendry was Fort Myers' very first bride, she also made numerous contributions to the town's settlement and early development. Laura was born in 1858, the eldest daughter and one of eight children born to Captain Francis Asbury—"F.A."—and Ardeline Ross Lanier Hendry. She came to live in Fort Myers 15 years later when her parents moved the family into one of the officers' quarters that had been part of the old Seminole Indian and Civil War fort. Moving next door to the town's earliest settlers, Joe and Christiana Vivas, the Hendrys became just the third family to make Fort Myers their home during the spring of 1873.

Not long after, a young man by the name of C.W. Thompson —"Waddy"—arrived. Waddy was a telegraph operator who had been sent to Fort Myers by the International Oceanic Telegraph Company to operate the station they were setting up there. Laura and Waddy met, fell madly in love and married on June 22, 1873, becoming the fledgling town's first bride and groom.

Laura went to work with her husband in the telegraph office. In time, she ran the station herself. She also advocated a number of causes, including that of the downtrodden Seminole Indians. She wrote numerous articles describing the injustices suffered by the Seminole nation at the hands of the State of Florida and the federal government that were published by east coast papers. She also played an instrumental role in organizing the Woman's Christian

Temperance Union (WCTU) in 1887, and fighting to prohibit the sale and consumption of alcohol in town.

When Lee County was formed, a vote was required to determine whether the county should be wet or dry. An election was scheduled on the issue for October 10, 1887. At that time, Fort Myers was a rowdy cow town where drovers, cow punchers and cattle brokers let off steam in the town's two saloons. Drunken fights often erupted, spilling into the streets. Laura and the WCTU waged a vigorous campaign, knocking on every door in town in their effort to amass enough votes to close the saloons and ban alcohol. For their part, the saloons sought to mobilize their patrons to prevent the county from going dry. But when the votes were counted, the drys had won convincingly, 117 to 67.

Sadly for Laura, her victory was short-lived. The ban on alcohol was lifted just two years later and would not be reinstated until 1908. By then, Laura had passed away, succumbing to tuberculosis in 1895. She was just 38 years old. According to the obituary that the *Fort Myers Press* ran the following day, Laura Hendry Thompson was "a woman of unusual force of character, keen perception and bright and active intellect, which made her a strong and earnest advocate of whatever cause she espoused."

Hendry family folklore states that F.A. Hendry named the town of LaBelle in honor of his daughters, Laura Jane and Carrie Belle. It was also F.A. who named Lee County in honor of his hero, General Robert E. Lee. LaBelle ultimately became the county seat of Hendry County after it ceded from Lee County and was created by the Florida Legislature in 1923.

Laura Jane Hendry and Waddy Thompson married in 1873, becoming the town's first bride and groom. (Courtesy of Southwest Florida Historical Society.)

SARAH KNIGHT TITUS

Offers Hospitality in Town's First Hotel

Sarah Kantz Knight Titus and her brother, Daniel Kantz, migrated from Pennsylvania to Fort Myers in 1882, arriving at the beginning of a great wave of gritty pioneers who settled in the town between 1882 and 1886. Shortly after coming to town, they built a two-story wood-frame hotel that they named The Keystone (the nickname of their home state), located just east of the business district. It was Fort Myers' first hotel, and the biggest social events in the community were held there for years.

When it was completed, The Keystone was touted as the finest hotel south of Tampa. It had an impressive parlor, 20 rooms for guests, a large dining room and a detached kitchen and wharf. Only two boarding houses offered any competition–the Frierson House and the Braman House.

Operating Fort Myers' only hotel for more than a decade is accomplishment enough, but Sarah also played a role in winning over the town's most famous winter resident, Thomas Edison. It happened during the winter of 1885.

The inventor had gone to Jacksonville for some much needed and well-deserved rest and relaxation, but the weather up there was a dreary mix of wind, rain and fog. Disgusted, Edison was preparing to return early to his laboratory in Menlo Park, New Jersey, when his friend and phonograph business partner, Ezra Gilliland, told him they should check out Fort Myers, where the weather was always nice. His curiosity appropriately piqued, Edison agreed and he, Gilliland and another friend hopped a train to Cedar Key, where they booked passage on a yacht named the *Jeannette*.

The *Jeannette* docked in Punta Rassa at the deep water wharf that served the Shultz Hotel, a huge frame structure that lumbered atop 14-foot pilings like an abandoned waterside barn. Built in 1864 by Union soldiers, the barracks had been taken over by the International Ocean Telegraph Company the year after the Civil War ended. The company's cable operator, George Shultz, had converted it into a quasi-hotel for cattlemen, travelers and, of late, anglers in search of highly prized tarpon. When Edison heard that there was a telegraph station upstairs, he went right inside where Shultz was only too happy to give the famous inventor a grand tour.

Historian Karl Grismer describes Shultz as "a jolly fellow who liked nothing better than to talk to friends." United by their common interest in telegraphy, the two men hit if off immediately. The next morning, Shultz regaled his inquisitive guest over cigars on the verandah with tales about the old Seminole Indian War outpost upriver called Fort Myers.

The next day, Edison arranged for the *Jeannette's* skipper, Captain Dan Paul, to take him upriver. Paul docked at the wharf of The Keystone, which Sarah Titus and her brother had recently renamed the Caloosa. There, Edison was treated to a generous helping of Sarah's brand of Pennsylvania Dutch hospitality. That evening, Edison strolled the village, mingling with the locals, who were thrilled to have such a celebrity in their midst. Edison was so impressed with Sarah and the townspeople that he put in an offer on a 13-acre parcel downriver the very next morning.

While there is admittedly no record or way of knowing just how big a role Sarah Titus played in disposing Edison to choose Fort

PETER OLIPHANT KNIGHT

Sarah Kantz Knight Titus' son, Peter Oliphant Knight, moved to Fort Myers in 1884, two years after his mother and uncle, and after receiving his law degree from Valparaiso University in Indiana at age 18. Like his mom, he got right to work in the emerging town. He helped to incorporate Fort Myers and was elected mayor before he turned 21. Interestingly, although he was one of the "founding fathers" who signed the call for election to incorporate, he was not allowed to vote to incorporate because he was under the age of 21! A couple of years later he was instrumental in the creation of Lee County and was named the first county attorney.

Following service in the Florida Legislature, Peter moved to Tampa in 1889 to start a law practice, five years after the city was chartered and when there were fewer than 1,000 residents. In addition to practicing law, he founded the area's present electric utility and a major bank, and became an influential member of Tampa's business and professional community for over 40 years. He was a founding partner in what is today the national law firm of Holland & Knight.

Myers as the location for his winter residence and botanical laboratory, there's no denying that she would have been one of the very first people that Edison met after stepping off the *Jeannette* on that March afternoon. And so she must be included along with bad weather in Jacksonville, Ezra Gilliland, and George Shultz when listing the factors that figured into Thomas Edison's decision to buy property in Fort Myers the following day.

Edison returned to Caloosa House the following year with his bride, Mina. A former Wisconsin schoolteacher by the name of Olive Stout came in on the same schooner. Stout was in town to check into the viability of the Fort Myers Press, which was up for sale. She was so impressed that she purchased the paper at first sight.

Mina, by contrast, was underwhelmed during her brief stay at Caloosa House while workmen put the finishing touches on Seminole Lodge. Because Fort Myers was virtually inaccessible by land, Edison had designed a two-story frame house the previous fall, had it pre-cut* in Maine, then shipped by water to Fort Myers for final assembly.

Edison referred to the Caloosa as a "flea trap," but Sarah held no grudge with him over the slight. She was one of 14 musicians who had banded together to form the town's first orchestra. In fact, she had hosted practice sessions in her home until her neighbors began complaining about the "hideous noise." Sarah and the band marched to Seminole Lodge once the newlyweds had settled in to serenade the deliriously happy couple. This time Mina was pleased. She was heard to effuse later that she had never heard such ethereal music.

As the town grew, Sarah Titus had the opportunity to welcome many other guests to Fort Myers. Like Edison and Olive Stout, a number of them made Fort Myers their permanent or winter home. Although Mary Hill opened her popular Hill House boarding home in 1889 and

*Coincidentally, or maybe not, an even earlier example of using pre-cut wood to build a house was the Lewis Miller Cottage at Lake Chautauqua.(See more on Chautauqua Institution in the chapter about Mina Miller Edison.) Nine years earlier, Miller had lumber cut to his specifications in Akron, Ohio and shipped overland for assembly as Chautauqua's first permanent home. Prior to this, tents had served as accommodations. Might Edison have got the idea from his father-in-law?

DANIEL KANTZ

Sarah's brother, Daniel Kantz, was one of the 45 "fathers" who voted on August 12, 1885 to incorporate the town and adopt a pineapple in full bloom as the official insignia of the town. (The pineapple was considered the fruit of fruits in the Land of the Caloosahatchee and almost every home had a pinery.) Daniel was part of the delegation of citizens who went to Key West for funds to rebuild the Fort Myers Academy after it burned down in 1886. He was principal of the school and was elected Lee County's first superintendent of public instruction in 1887. He was also a member of the Fort Myers Dramatic Society and was a member of the cast of its first production, *Lady Audrey's Secret*.

Louis Hendry followed with the 14-room Hendry House in 1890, the Caloosa remained the only hotel in town until 1898. Then New York department store magnate Hugh O'Neill welcomed the public into his 50-room Fort Myers Hotel, which he renamed the Royal Palm Hotel a short time later. By then, Sarah and her brother had made some changes of their own.

In 1891 Sarah married George Washington—"Wash"—Hendry, a county judge in Fort Myers, and brother of F.A. and Marion. George had settled in Polk County, but moved to Fort Myers around 1890 as a recent widower. Records indicate that George was in Fort Myers only three or four years, but Sarah remained in Fort Myers.

Meanwhile, the town was growing in the opposite direction of the Caloosa, and Sarah and Daniel correctly determined that they needed to be closer to the downtown business district if they were going to remain competitive with Hill House, Hendry House and any new hotels that might come along. So in 1895, they hired a local contractor to pick up their hotel and move it to the corner of First and Monroe, where the City of Palms Parking Garage is located today. At the same time, they decided to give the Caloosa a new name, The Fort Myers Inn.

A few years later, Sarah and Daniel sold the hotel to Dr. W.S. Turner. He enlarged it and changed the name to the Riverside Hotel, but Sarah Knight Titus will forever hold a place of distinction among Fort Myers' female hoteliers, a distinguished group that included Mrs. Louis Lanier, Mary Florence Hill and Tootie McGregor Terry.

The June 18, 1903 edition of *The Tampa Tribune* reported that Sarah (Mrs. G.W. Hendry) died at the age of 61.

Author note: The year after Sarah passed away, George Washington Hendry married Annie Hughes in Polk County.

JULIA ALLEN HANSON

A Refining Influence in a "Straggly Pioneer Village"

She was known as the "Most Beloved Woman in Florida" and the "Mother of all Women's Clubs." She was identified with practically every forward-looking movement in South Florida for more than 50 years. In 1885, she co-founded the Fort Myers Woman's Club along with Olive Stout, Flossie Hill and Florida Heitman, serving as the organization's president and guiding force for 29 years. Although those who knew her in later life marveled at her silver mane and the keen twinkle in her inquisitive eyes, she was once described in English publications as one of the "most beautiful titian haired girls in all England." Her name was Julia Allen Hanson, and she left an indelible imprint on Fort Myers during her half century in our town.

Julia Allen was born in London, England in 1843 to a well-known and accomplished architect whose credits included designing the approaches to the London Bridge. Part of British high society, she was intimately acquainted with such famous figures as the Duke of Wellington, Charles Dickens, Lord Tennyson, Anthony Trollope, Prince Arthur, the Duke of Devonshire and Florence Nightingale. Byrne-Jones and Sir John Millais both painted portraits of her.

From British high society to tiny cow town
She came to the United States in 1880 after marrying noted physi-

cian and surgeon William Hanson. Four years later, the couple discovered the tiny cow town called Fort Myers on their way to Cuba and decided to settle here instead.

Her first order of business after settling in was to establish a church in the town. To accomplish the feat, she fostered two Episcopal women's organizations in order to raise the funds needed to build the church.

"But her enthusiasm and ability extended to other fields," the *Fort Myers News-Press* noted in Hanson's 1934 obituary, "and she was identified with organizing the first local chapter of the National Woman's Christian Temperance Union (WCTU), the Woman's Club, the Friday Musicale, the Palmetto Society, the first reading association (which became the progenitor of the public library), the Cemetery Improvement Association, the first Lee Memorial Hospital Association, the first Sunday school, and the first Federation of Women's Clubs."

She also founded the first Needlework Guild and for many years was chairwoman of the Seminole Welfare Committee of the Florida Federation of Clubs. She was a Deputy Commissioner of the Florida Game and Fish Department and was recognized by the United States Audubon Society as a writer and artist on the subject of bird life in Florida. She was also instrumental in the passage of many laws for the protection of bird life and the care of the Seminoles.

A refining influence

In fact, Julia Allen Hanson played such an important role in the development of South Florida that the 1914-15 *Women's Who's Who of America* devoted

Julia's husband, Dr. William Hanson, distinguished himself during his time in Fort Myers as Thomas Edison's personal physician and doctor to the Seminole Indians who had avoided deportation to Oklahoma. He also became a real estate developer, opening one of the town's first subdivisions. But it was the couple's son, W. Stanley Hanson, who became best known for his work among the Seminoles, and his advocacy on their behalf and for preservation of their tribal identity and cultural heritage.

Julia Allen Hanson, known as the "Most Beloved Woman in Florida," left an indelible imprint on Fort Myers. (Courtesy of Hanson Family Archives.)

several paragraphs to reporting her many activities. "Besides being well known as a writer, artist and speaker," the *News-Press* summarized, "Mrs. Hanson played the role of 'mother' to everybody and everything in Fort Myers and her refined influence was of great importance in the formative stages of the pioneer community."

"For half a century, she was so influential in community affairs that it is difficult to imagine what Fort Myers would have been without her progressive influence," notes local historian Gerri Reaves in her tome, *Legendary Locals of Fort Myers.*

"Fort Myers has had some famous characters, good, bad and indifferent," the *News-Press* wrote in the concluding paragraphs of Julia's obituary. "There was the roaring cowboy, Dennis Sheridan, slain in a street scene during his tough moments by the mild-mannered, soft spoken, stout-hearted city marshal, L.M. Stroup. There was Captain F.A. Hendry, the benevolent leader of pioneer times, and the broad-shouldered Captain 'Bill' Towles, strong man of a later date. There was Colonel Peter O. Knight, who was the spark plug of the village when a youth of 18, and Stafford C. Cleveland, the erudite and eminent editor who, at three score years, uprooted himself from the solid country of western New York to come and start a backwoods newspaper. And there was Mrs. Julia A. Hanson, who lived and sparkled among these and other mighty men of the times from that day to yesterday. Like the most virile of them, she left her mark on the community. She came here in the mid-eighties, the bride of the late Dr. William Hanson. A ravishing beauty, she had been painted by famous artists and toasted by the gallants of England. Reared among gentlefolk and educated in the culture of the world's highest civilization, she found herself a matron in the maturity of middle age, plumped down in a straggly pioneer village in the tropical wilds of South Florida .... [S]he helped, as much as any other, to endow Fort Myers with the charm which captivates all newcomers. Through her knowledge, and by her interest, she promoted the culture of the town from the day of her arrival in the lusty past to the times as recent as her final illness."

MINA MILLER EDISON

"Home Executive," Dedicated
Conservationist, Community Improver

Mina Miller was born July 6, 1865, seventh of 11 children of a successful inventor and wealthy manufacturer of farm tools, as well as Chautauqua Institution co-founder, Lewis Miller (see Author note, p. 46). After graduating from high school with honors, she traveled for a year in Europe, then studied music and the classics at Miss Johnson's Ladies' Seminary, a finishing school located in Boston. It was here that Mina was introduced to the newly widowed Thomas Edison by mutual friends Ezra and Lillian Gilliland.

According to biographer Matthew Josephson, Mina "staggered" Edison. In contrast to the legion of fawning women that the matchmaking Gillilands had paraded before Edison, Mina was not only young and beautiful, she was poised and self-confident, even in the presence of such a world-renowned figure. At the time, Edison was keeping a diary, and wrote this entry, which aptly sums up his growing feelings for the beguiling Miss Miller: "Saw a lady who looked like Mina. Got thinking about Mina and came near being run over by a street car. If Mina interferes much more, will have to take out an accident policy."

The couple married in 1886 at the Miller family home in Akron, Ohio, roughly one year after first meeting. Edison brought his new bride to Fort Myers, where they honeymooned at Sarah Knight Titus and Daniel Kantz's Keystone Hotel while their winter home, Seminole Lodge, was being completed. Edison had purchased the 13-acre riverfront estate from cattleman Samuel Summerlin the year before.

Despite a nearly 20-year age difference, Thomas Edison and Mina were a harmonious match, and had deep respect and love for each other. Since childhood, Mina had spent the month of August every year at Chautauqua, so she had been around highly educated people, some famous, all her life. Mina's education and social status served her well as the young wife of an internationally famous inventor.

As Edison supervised his "muckers" down the hill at home back in Glenmont, New Jersey, Mina—self-described "home executive"—hired and supervised a staff of maids, a cook, a nanny and a gardening staff. She also became an important asset to her husband's business, essentially serving as his one-person public relations department. After 1891 she, not her husband, owned the house, a strategic move designed to protect the house from being seized to pay the entrepreneurial Edison's debts should he ever find it necessary to declare bankruptcy.

Edison already had three children from his marriage to Mary Stillwell, and Mina and Thomas Edison had three children of their own. While all of Edison's children married, only Madeleine, his oldest child with Mina, had children of her own. Despite it being unusual in those days for girls to attend college, even girls from wealthy or prominent families, Madeleine attended Bryn Mawr College in Pennsylvania for two years and was a good student. She then ran for the Republican nomination for U.S. Congress and lost, but

Mina and Thomas Edison shared a sense of purpose and had a deep respect and love for each other. (Courtesy of Edison & Ford Winter Estates.)

After graduating from high school with honors, Mina Miller traveled for a year in Europe, then studied music and the classics at a finishing school in Boston. (Courtesy of Edison & Ford Winter Estates.)

it was a close race. Madeleine and her husband, John Eyre Sloane, had four sons, who all had Edison for their middle name.

Both of the Edisons' sons, Charles and Theodore, graduated from Massachusetts Institute of Technology. Charles went into business administration and became president of his father's industries, Thomas A. Edison, Incorporated. He later moved into politics and eventually became Secretary of the Navy and also served as Governor of New Jersey. Theodore, Edison's youngest child and the only one to follow in his father's footsteps, graduated with a degree in physics and earned several patents during his career as a mechanical engineer. He was also a philanthropist and expert in conservation.

Mina comes into her own

As Mina's children grew up and moved from home, Mina came into her own. She became active in numerous social welfare movements including the Chautauqua Association (where she served as president of the Bird & Tree Club), the American Red Cross, the West Orange (New Jersey) Community League, the National Audubon Society, the local Methodist church, the John Burroughs Association, the Daughters of the American Revolution (where she served for a year as its national chaplain), and the School Garden Association of America. In Fort Myers, Mina was instrumental in the foundation of the Fort Myers Round Table, a group of local leaders whom she brought together around the dining room table at Seminole Lodge to discuss, make and implement plans for community improvement.

She gave numerous speeches to local groups in West Orange and in Fort Myers, often on the importance of garden clubs and neighborhood organizations, the role of recreation in the education of children, and the value of musical instruction. She started the Periwinkle Garden Club, now the oldest garden club in Lee County. A dedicated conservationist long before that word became part of our everyday lexicon, she became

Mina's belief in the importance of healthful habits and activities for the physical and cultural well-being of individuals and communities is summarized in her closing remarks in a talk to the National Recreation Congress in the late 1920s.

We are facing a vast challenge, but I believe it can and will be met. I like to look ahead to the time when every American city and town and county district will have better opportunities for more and better play; will enjoy leisure time pursuits that build up the body and minister to the mind and spirit. One of the most important things this group can do is show our young people that the best things in life are free; that they may be had without paying a cent. Bring our children closer to the simple and the fundamental; help them to discover hobbies that they may keep all their lives; train their hands and their hearts to the joy of creating perfect things; hold up to them ideals of fine sportsmanship—and we will have a better nation tomorrow.

a potent force for the conservation movement in the U.S. The rapid growth of cities in the 1930s and their encroachment of pristine areas was a major concern, and Mina most likely had input in the great movement that emerged to preserve wild areas. She became close friends with and an ardent supporter of Jay "Ding" Darling, the renowned cartoonist turned conservationist who was tapped by President Franklin Delano Roosevelt in 1934 to head the U.S. Biological Survey (forerunner of the U.S. Fish and Wildlife Service).

After her husband's death in 1931, Mina's community involvement continued. She married childhood friend Edward Hughes in 1935, but after his death in 1940, Mina resumed using Edison as her surname. When the Thomas Alva Edison Foundation was formed in 1946 "for the advancement of education and scientific research," Mina became its honorary chair. A year later, she graciously deeded Seminole Lodge and the rest of the winter estate to the City of Fort Myers in order to perpetuate Edison's name and fame. She died shortly thereafter at the age of 82, and is buried beside Thomas Edison on the grounds of their home in New Jersey.

Author note: The Chautauqua Institution is a not-for-profit educational center in southwestern New York State. Originally called the Chautauqua Lake Sunday School Assembly, the Institution was founded in 1874 by Lewis Miller and John Heyl Vincent as an educational experiment in out-of-school, vacation learning. Immediately successful, it quickly broadened beyond courses for Sunday school teachers to include academic subjects, music, art and physical education.

Now ecumenical in spirit and practice, since the Institution's founding the Chautauqua philosophy has been that everyday life should integrate leisure, education, fine arts, and spirituality. Courses in art, music, dance, theater, and writing skills are offered during its nine-week summer season.

OLIVE STOUT

Smooths Out Young Town's Rough Edges

Olive Elizabeth Stout first heard of Fort Myers while she and her husband, Frank, were living in Central Florida. Frank had taken a job with a publication called the *Agriculturalist*, but he was in the market for something he could call his own. Apparently there was a little newspaper for sale in a growing town on the west coast of Florida, and Olive took off to check out the town and attendant business opportunity.

Olive was not a newspaper reporter or editor herself. She had been a schoolteacher back home in Wisconsin, where she met Frank, a newspaperman who had relocated from his home state of Michigan. The two married in 1869 and soon moved to Kansas, where Frank started one paper and served as associate publisher for another. But Frank's aspirations were undermined by poor health, and the couple moved to Florida to take advantage of its more temperate climate. They had heard that the weather was supposed to be even nicer in Fort Myers.

Thomas Edison no doubt confirmed that fact for Olive on the ride to Fort Myers. He and his bride, Mina, were passengers on the same steamer that brought Olive to town in March of 1886. The weather is what had attracted Edison to the area the year before. The friendly townspeople had been what inspired him to find a realtor and buy 13 acres on the wide, slow-flowing Caloosahatchee

River. He was in the process of having a winter home and botanical laboratory erected on the property.

By the time she set foot on the wharf of the Keystone Hotel, Olive was understandably predisposed to buy *The Press* if its profitability panned out at all. The paper was barely 15 months old. In fact, the paper's editor, Stafford Cleveland,* had intended to set up shop in Fort Ogden to the north. But when the skipper of the schooner that was bringing him down the coast learned that he had a bona fide newspaper editor on board along with his printing press, he took him straight to Fort Myers so that the town leaders could prevail upon him to publish his paper there instead.

No sooner had the boat docked than the town's leaders turned out in force to pitch the merits of publishing a newspaper in Fort Myers. Venerable cattle-man and founder Captain F.A. Hendry guaranteed Cleveland 300 subscribers during the paper's first year. Horticulturalist and Fort Myers booster W.P. Gardner offered to cover the first $600 of Cleveland's expenses. Leading citizen Howell Parker, realtor C.J. Huelsenkamp, and merchant Taylor Frierson prom-ised to become regular advertisers. Ed Evans and Carl Roberts even agreed to set up Cleveland's plant free of charge. Overwhelmed, Cleveland happily consented, beginning a love affair between the town and its only newspaper that was unexpectedly cut short when the 63-year-old editor died suddenly in December of 1885 of Bright's disease. Now the town was eager for a quali-fied newspaperman like Frank Stout to rescue the paper, Cleveland's widow told Olive. Although the town's population only numbered in the hundreds, Olive purchased the publication at first sight. Fort Myers was on the move, and Olive Stout intended to be part of it.

Olive seizes the moment

Between 1882 and 1886, Fort Myers grew more than during the 17 years that followed the end of the Civil War. Frank and Olive arrived at the tail end of a wave of influential pioneers that included such luminaries as Captain William A. Towles, W.P. and Bertie Gardner, Dr. William and Julia Hanson, T.E. and Taff Langford, Edward and Thomas Evans, the Jeffcoat brothers, Robert A. Henderson, Carl F. Roberts, the brothers Travers, Reinhold Kinzie, C.T. Tooke, and Daniel Kantz and his sister, Sarah Knight Titus. Every one of these new-

---

Ironically, Fort Myers' busiest and most important thoroughfare is named in honor of Stafford Cleveland even though he only served as editor of the Fort Myers Press for a little more than a year. No street of any size or significance bears Olive Stout's name in spite of her affiliation with the News-Press for more than 27 years and her numerous contributions to the town's culture, beautification and heritage between her arrival in 1886 and death 44 years later.

comers was destined to make significant contributions to the town's early development and their names figure prominently in the history of Fort Myers. And thanks to Olive's swift decision, she and Frank would be on hand to record and report on it all.

Frank and Olive took over the *Fort Myers Press* in May of 1886. In the months that followed, they applied themselves to building the paper into a highly regarded and successful business. While Olive worked with Frank at the paper, she also began to pursue a number of her own civic, charitable and political causes.

"The year 1889 was a huge year for Great-Grandmother," said Bryon Stout in an interview several years ago. "She raised the money to build St. Luke's Episcopal Church adjacent to her home and was appointed postmaster by President William McKinley." Appointed in 1889, Olive would hold that office until 1893. She was re-appointed to the position by President Teddy Roosevelt in 1897, and served in that capacity until 1906.

While 1889 may have marked a high point for Olive, the ensuing decade proved turbulent as a result of her husband's political views. Back in Wisconsin and Kansas, Frank had been an ardent Republican. But Fort Myers was passionately Democratic and the newspaper's advertisers and readers would not even abide neutrality when it came to political reporting, never mind a Republican bent. In an effort to placate the townsfolk, Stout hired a political editor. That seemed to work out fairly well for a time, but then the editor improvidently decided to take on F.A. and the powerful Hendry faction for having too much influence in the town's political and judicial machinery. The

Artist Africa Valdez's portrait of Olive Stout at three different stages of life. (Courtesy of the artist.)

Olive Stout purchased the *Fort Myers Press* at first sight in 1886. Fort Myers was on the move, and she intended to be part of it! (Courtesy of Southwest Florida Historical Society.)

Hendrys wasted no time. They retaliated by backing a competing publication. Both papers lost money and Frank had to sell the *Press*. He got it back when the buyer could not make a success of it either, but he had to yield the editorship when the two papers agreed to consolidate early in 1897.

Although Frank was damaged goods, Olive continued to enjoy a good reputation which she took advantage of in June of 1900 when she partnered with Flossie Hill, Florida Heitman and Julia Hanson to form the Fort Myers Woman's Club.

The Fort Myers Woman's Club—now known as the Woman's Community Club—was organized in Olive's living room and she was elected its first president. Given the tumult of the preceding decade, the members passed a resolution forbidding political or social discussions "to make sure that the club meetings wouldn't end up in hair pulling," quips historian Karl Grismer in *The Story of Fort Myers*. But in time, the Woman's Club became one of the strongest organizations in the city "and the members, disregarding the resolution they had passed, took a leading part in public affairs, helping greatly to make Fort Myers the city it is today," Grismer concludes.

One of the first initiatives that the Woman's Club pursued was the creation of a public reading room. It opened in March 1903 in a small storefront on the northeast corner of First and Hendry Streets. Club members and winter residents donated books, magazines and newspapers. The club had to vacate the space in November 1904 when real estate developer Harvie Heitman began clearing land for the Bradford Hotel. The reading room re-opened in February 1906 in a small building on the southwest corner of First and Jackson that had previously been used as a law office. Olive Stout served as the first librarian. Later she alternated in this capacity with other club members.

Many blights to remove!

Olive also played a role in getting the cows off the streets of Fort Myers. It was a cause that Olive's husband, Frank, had espoused as far back as 1887, when he lamented in an editorial in the *Press*, "We want a court house, we want hotels, we want improvements of all kinds. But what encouragement is it to a person to buy and improve his property when he awakes in the morning to find his yard a mass of filth and torn up by the feet of cattle that find pasturage in our public streets and yards?"

Frank had to abandon his efforts to ban free-roaming cattle when the Hendrys, other local cattlemen, and their friends objected to his entreaties. But in 1907, Olive banded together with nine other women for purposes of ridding the town's streets of the four-legged nuisances. They called themselves the Civic League and Olive Stout served as its first president. So effective were their efforts that by September of 1908 they had succeeded in convincing the town council to pass and enforce an ordinance requiring that all cattle and milk cows be penned up once and for all.

Olive and the Civic League next led a movement to beautify the city by planting trees along the streets. They hired workers to clean the streets until the city finally assumed responsibility for this function, and they began purchasing street benches, selling advertising on them to defray their cost. But there was one more blight in the business district that Olive still needed to remove.

"When she arrived in Fort Myers," recounts Bryon Stout, "First Street was a notorious row of saloons where cowboys rode roughshod and fights often spilled into the streets." Another of the town's pioneering women, Laura Hendry Thompson, had helped organize the Woman's Christian Temperance Union and had led a bitter door-to-door campaign that culminated with the prohibition on the sale and consumption of alcohol in 1887. But the ban had not stuck and by 1890, Fort Myers and the county as a whole were wet once again. No stranger to controversial causes, Olive teamed up with the WCTU in 1908 and brought in the famous radical member of the temperance movement, Carrie Nation, to lead a new campaign to ban alcohol in the town. The drys won again, and this time the sale of alcohol was banned until Prohibition was repealed nationwide 25 years later.

Olive had one last campaign to wage. On January 2, 1912, representatives from all of the town's civic organizations, churches, businesses and professionals convened to discuss a pressing issue: The town had no hospital. People who became critically injured or ill had to be transported to Tampa or Key West or cared for at home. A working committee was established, and although she was not appointed as an official member, Olive attended the committee's meetings.

It took four years and County Commission Chairman William A. Towles' late night dismantling of the old courthouse to provide the wood needed for its construction, but the Lee County Hospital was finally built. It opened in 1916 with Olive serving on the hospital Board of Directors along with Chairman Carl F. Roberts and Dr. W.B. Winkler, Mrs. Harry Laycock (daughter-in-law of Mary Laycock), Miss Cordelia Nutt, Minnie Gardner and Julia Hanson.

Olive Stout died in 1930 at the age of 83 leaving, in the estimation of the *Fort Myers News-Press*, "a record as one of those tireless frontier women determined to take the rough edges off one of America's cow towns."

FLOSSIE HILL

Firefighter and Fashionista

When Mary Hill arrived from Alabama in 1889 with her daughters Flossie and Annie, she discovered that there was a dearth of lodging in Fort Myers for newcomers like herself and tourists like the Edisons, McGregors and others who made the trip upriver from Punta Rassa. At the time, the only accommodations in town were at the Keystone, a two-story, 20-room frame hotel with a large dining room, impressive parlor, detached kitchen and wharf.

Needing to establish an income stream from which to support herself and her daughters, Mary opened a small boarding house on the southwest corner of First and Lee, where the Franklin Arms luxury condominiums are located today.

Because Annie suffered from a chronic illness and was always in poor health, Flossie helped her mother run the boarding house. Over the ensuing years, they kept pace with competing boarding houses and hotels, adding rooms and becoming one of the most popular hostelries in town. In the process, Flossie gained a well-deserved reputation as a take-charge kind of woman. For example, when the men in town decided to while away their spare time playing sandlot baseball, Flossie teamed up with friends Olive Stout, Julia Hanson and Florida Heitman to found the Fort Myers Woman's Club, for which Flossie served as recording secretary. Taking a leadership role in public affairs some 20 years before women won the right to vote or could hold public office, the Woman's Club discussed current events, music and domestic questions, initiated civic beautification projects, and laid the groundwork for the town's public library system.

Flossie leads a fire brigade

Flossie's leadership qualities also served the town well when the business district nearly burned to the ground during the great fire of 1903. To hear historians tell the tale, you'd think that the volunteer firefighters and a nearby railroad construction crew saved the town from certain destruction. But it was actually a group of women led by Flossie Hill who rescued Fort Myers from the same fate that Chicago suffered in its great fire of 1871.

The fire started on Friday, October 16 in a two-story, wood-frame building on the corner of Hendry and Oak (now Main) Streets. Property owner Carl Roberts operated a mortuary and woodworking business on the ground floor and maintained his personal residence on the floor above. The fire most likely started in a defective flue.

A brisk wind was blowing out of the southwest that morning, and Flossie may have smelled the smoke even before she heard the alarm go out. Either way, she probably didn't give it a second thought. After all, fires were nothing new in Fort Myers. Besides, the town now had a crack volunteer fire department and a fine second-hand fire pump dubbed "old Andrew Jackson," along with a hook and ladder, hose cart and 250 feet of hose. Chief Cates and the firefighters would have the fire out in no time at all.

Flossie Hill's natural leadership qualities served the town well on more than one occasion. (Courtesy of Southwest Florida Historical Society.)

Flossie Hill opened Fort Myers' first department store in 1905. When she died in 1956 she bequeathed stock in her store to the employees who had been with her more than 20 years. (Courtesy of Southwest Florida Museum of History.)

Ironically, Carl Roberts had served briefly as the chief before Cates, and he'd made space available in his building for the volunteers and their equipment. Now, smoke was billowing from the roof of Roberts' building and by the time the volunteers arrived on the scene, the entire second story was fully engulfed in flames. Somehow they managed to get their equipment out of the burning building, but when they hooked up the pump to the artesian well in the intersection of Hendry and First, a block away, a valve stuck and the panicked men had to take the pump down to the river to free it up.

Meanwhile, wind-whipped burning embers ignited the M.N. Verner store 75 feet away. A second alarm went out to summon every available man, woman and child within the sound of the fire bell. People came running from every direction and quickly formed a bucket brigade. Heitman's Livery Stable caught fire next, followed by Taff Langford's home, Gilliam's store, Hopson's livery and Charles Braman's home. No sooner did the townspeople put out these fires than the fire jumped the street, with the Evans warehouse erupting in flames. At this point, historian Karl Grismer reports, "merchants everywhere in the business district began removing their goods as the situation looked hopeless."

About this time, the volunteers got the pump working, but by the time they raced back from the river and hooked it up, they were too exhausted to man the pump, which required 30 men to operate. That's when Flossie Hill stepped to the forefront and rallied her friends to take over for the spent volunteers. Switchboard operator Alice Hendry Tooke McCann quickly joined her, followed by Mrs. Stroup (wife of Larkin Moses Stroup, the town's marshal) and her daughters, Bessie Thorpe, Josie Hendry, and Laura and Lillian Gonzalez. Although they too were quickly tiring, they almost had the fire extinguished when a construction crew came running into town and shooed Flossie and her cohorts away. The men, who had been working on the railroad two miles away, put out the rest of the flames. But it was Flossie and her friends who stopped the fire from spreading to a row of nearby wood buildings even if it was the construction workers who got credit for putting out the last of the flames.

Flossie opens first department store

In 1905, Flossie decided to branch out, opting to open Fort Myers' first department store. It was a bold move. Besides Flossie having scant experience in buying and selling merchandise, the total population of the town was only slightly more than 4,000 men, women and children. Known as The Ladies Trading Place, the M. Flossie Hill Department Store operated at various locations–all within a block of Bay and Jackson. To illustrate just how small the town was during this period of time, telephone numbers were just two digits long. When it was located at 1016 First Street in the 1940s, the exchange for The Ladies Trading Place was Phone 51.

Although the store consumed vast amounts of her time, Flossie also continued to help her mother operate the Hill House. Flossie was there on April 15, 1907 when fire once again threatened the business district. This fire started in another of Carl Roberts' buildings, a three-story, wood-frame building located directly across Lee Street from the Hill House Hotel, and by the time the city's new Watrous gas fire truck pulled up to the structure, its top two floors were burning furiously. This time, the wind was blowing out of the east and the business district found itself in peril again since, aside from Harvie Heitman's brick building on Jackson, the Bradford Hotel and the Stone Block Building on First and Hendry, all the other buildings were framed, sided and shingled with incendiary wood. And the building in the most danger was the Hill House. But the volunteers saved the Hill House and the rest of the town, and life went on.

In 1916, Flossie and her mother decided it was time to completely renovate Hill House. Recalling their close call nine years earlier, they tore down the two-story balustrade building and replaced it with a 50 by 80-foot brick and stucco structure that had 26 steam-heated rooms, most equipped with their own bath.

The renovations made Hill House more competitive with the other hotels in town, which included the much larger Bradford, the Royal Palm Hotel (which only offered a bath on each floor), the Cottage Home, Riverview, the Kenmore, the newly completed Graystone and retired Michigan banker Peter Tonnelier's Hotel de Leon in the old Stone Block Building, the first of four medium-sized hotels he would open in Fort Myers. But as Flossie's name was on the construction contract, it is also possible, if not likely, that the improvements were designed to augment the establishment's curb appeal and profitability in contemplation of its sale. Sure enough, Mary sold the Hill House two years later to local hardware magnate W. P. Franklin, who promptly changed the Hill House's name to the Franklin Arms Hotel.

Flossie operated the M. Flossie Hill Department Store for half a century. Always forward-thinking, when Flossie died in 1956, she bequeathed stock in her store to the employees who had been with her more than 20 years. Those employees continued Flossie's legacy for more than a decade. After Sears & Roebuck moved to the Edison Mall in 1963, Harvie Heitman's daughter, Lorraine Blownstine, renovated the Heitman brick building and added an elevator, in order to accommodate The Ladies Trading Place. But downtown merchants found it increasingly difficult to compete with the Mall, and The Ladies Trading Place followed Sears & Roebuck to the mall a few years later, where it was eventually acquired by a large chain department store.

Ironically, today everyone mentions Flossie's men's clothing store counterpart, Sidney Davis, but until now, the story of Flossie Hill and The Ladies Trading Place is largely unknown.

TOOTIE MCGREGOR TERRY

The Woman Who Changed Fort Myers' Look and Landscape Forever

Of all the people who influenced the early development of Fort Myers, none left a greater imprint on the town than Tootie McGregor Terry. Tootie almost single-handedly changed the topography of the town by convincing property owners to install a seawall along the riverfront and the city to finally pave its weed-strewn, shell and sand roads. As a hotelier, she created luxury accommodations that enticed numerous millionaires, celebrities and businessmen to the area who then made significant contributions to the town's identity, economy and culture. Tootie also brought golf and Major League Baseball to Fort Myers.

But if it had not been for an intrepid angler who fished the waters of Punta Rassa in 1885, Tootie and her husband, Ambrose McGregor, may have never come to Southwest Florida at all.

On the morning of March 12, 1885, New York sportsman W. H. Wood set out from the Shultz Hotel in the deep water shipping port of Punta Rassa with a rod and reel determined to snag himself a tarpon. The other guests at the converted Civil War Army barracks thought that Wood had lost his mind. Everyone knew the only way to catch a tarpon was with a harpoon or, possibly, a shark hook attached to a chain line. But the Silver King that took the mullet offered up by Wood as bait did not know that. The 93-pound tarpon ran half a mile, leaping out of the sea green water time after time in its desperate effort to spit out Wood's crude cod "o" hook.

But 26 minutes later, Wood boated the exhausted 5-foot 9-inch fish, making angling history, putting Southwest Florida on the sport fishing map, and piquing the interest of oil baron Ambrose M. McGregor and his wife Tootie (née Jerusha Barber).

By the year 1892, Tootie and Ambrose had built a life rich in social and family connections, as well as business success, in their hometown of Cleveland, Ohio. With Tootie's support and assistance, Ambrose had risen through the ranks at Standard Oil Company, then the largest oil refiner in the world, starting as a refinery foreman and eventually becoming president and CEO. But the Scotsman's success was tempered by the poor health of the couple's only child, Bradford. So when the boy's physician recommended that Ambrose and Tootie take their son to Florida for the winter, they headed straight for George Shultz's aptly renamed Tarpon House to try their hand at tarpon fishing.

On an off-day that February, the McGregors sailed up the pristine waters of the Caloosahatchee River to have a look at the nearby town of Fort Myers. They must have been astonished by what they found when they first set foot on the long rough-hewn pine wharf the Army had built in 1852. In stark contrast to their hometown, Fort Myers consisted of just two uneven rows of cheaply constructed clapboard-over-wood-frame storefronts that housed saloons, livery stables, blacksmith shops and general stores.

Tootie and Ambrose had to pick their way through the unpaved, ungraded sandy stretches that connected the buildings, being careful to avoid the tangles of weeds, wagon wheel ruts and free-roaming cattle and hogs that gave resi-

Ambrose McGregor (Courtesy of Southwest Florida Historical Society.)

No one did more to foster Fort Myers' growth and early development than Jerusha Barber "Tootie" McGregor Terry. (Courtesy of Southwest Florida Historical Society.)

dents fits of anguish and anger. Not only did Fort Myers have no paved roads, sidewalks or street lights, it had no phone or electrical service, running water or sanitary system. Thick, black hordes of mosquitoes bred in the cisterns and shallow wells used to collect water, inflicting "chills and fever" (malaria) on the unsuspecting locals. Residents were also subject to dysentery as a consequence of contamination from nearby privies. But the weather was incredible, the fishing abundant and the pace so easy that the McGregors fell in love with the town and its 900 friendly residents. They decided on the spot to make Fort Myers their winter home.

They sought out a local realtor, who had just the place in mind for an important and wealthy businessman and his industrious wife. He took Ambrose and Tootie to see the half of Seminole Lodge for sale by E.T. Gilliland.

It had been Gilliland who had informed Thomas Edison about the tiny burgh of Fort Myers in 1885 when bad weather in Jacksonville nearly sent the inventor packing for his Menlo Park laboratory. It was Gilliland as well who had introduced the lonely widower to beautiful socialite Mina Miller, who would quickly become the second Mrs. Edison. In reciprocity, Edison had designed and built two homes out of Maine lumber on the 13-acre spread he purchased in 1885 along the banks of the Caloosahatchee—one for Gilliland and the other for himself. But Edison had caught Gilliland skimming from their phonograph business and severed all ties with him, and now the embarrassed Gilliland was eager to dispose of his half of the lodge.

Several months after Tootie's death, Marshall Terry asked the city council for permission to install a fountain to memorialize his wife and all she had done to transform Fort Myers from the rough and tumble cow town she and Ambrose had discovered in 1892 into the highly regarded winter resort she left behind at the time of her death. The Tootie McGregor Fountain was dedicated on the first anniversary of Tootie's death at Five Points, the intersection where the new McGregor Boulevard would meet Cleveland Avenue, Anderson Avenue (now Martin Luther King, Jr. Boulevard), Carson and Main Streets. While the fountain was relocated to the Fort Myers Country Club on McGregor in the 1950s to make way for the approach to the bridge to North Fort Myers, it remains a cherished part of and the oldest work in Fort Myers' public art collection. No one—male or female—did more to foster Fort Myers' growth and early development than Jerusha Barber "Tootie" McGregor Terry. (Photo courtesy of Southwest Florida Historical Society.)

Ambrose McGregor struck a deal to buy Gilliland's half of the estate for the modest sum of $4,000. The sale closed in July 1892.

However, Tom and Mina Edison were not frequenting Seminole Lodge in 1892. In fact, they had last visited Seminole Lodge in the spring of 1887–some locals claimed that the Edisons had been scared off by an outbreak of yellow fever that struck Key West and Tampa in May of that year. In any case, the Edisons' absence did not deter the McGregors. They moved into their half of Seminole Lodge that December and began making improvements to their new winter home.

Grief propels Tootie's social and civic activism

In 1894, Tootie, Ambrose and Bradford were basking in the afterglow of their third Christmas at the lodge when, on the morning of December 29, the mercury plunged to a bone-chilling 24 degrees. Known ever after as The Big Freeze, the cold spell destroyed or damaged millions of citrus trees in the upper and middle portions of the state. Those that survived were killed off seven weeks later when an even colder blast of polar air swept down the peninsula. But not a single tree in or around Fort Myers was affected by the cold temperatures. When wiped-out growers in other parts of Florida learned this, they began snapping up local groves and large tracts of land throughout Lee County (Lee included Hendry and Collier counties at the time).

Ambrose McGregor was not one to miss out on a lucrative business opportunity, and he too purchased two large parcels and immediately planted groves of orange and grapefruit trees. Predicting exponential growth for the town and surrounding areas, he went on to invest $150,000 in 32 properties during the next few years, becoming one of the town's largest land owners in the process. During this time, he also formed a strategic relationship with an up-and-coming store owner and real estate developer, Harvie E. Heitman, financing the first brick building to be erected in the tinderbox town.

Sadly, Ambrose died of stomach cancer in 1900 at the age of 58. Tragedy struck Tootie again two years later when Bradford died of reported kidney disease just two days after marrying his high school sweetheart, Florence Quintard. With husband and son both gone, there was nothing holding Tootie to Fort Myers. Ambrose had left Tootie a very wealthy widow. With

Tootie did not forget her native Cleveland. She partnered with her sister, Sophia Barber McCrosky, to found one of that city's first private nursing homes. The sisters conceived it as a place for "gentlewomen who could no longer care for themselves." Also named for Ambrose, the A.M. McGregor Home was incorporated in 1904, opened in 1908 with 25 residents, and still serves Ohio's elderly.

stock in Standard Oil valued at $16 million and dividend income of $1.5 million annually, Tootie was reputed to be the tenth wealthiest person in the United States and richest woman in the country. She could have returned to Cleveland or moved to Manhattan or even London or Paris. But she shared Ambrose's passion for the frontier town and his commitment to Fort Myers' future. So she stayed. More, she transformed her grief into social and civic activism—a mindset she inherited from her father, who had been a judge in Cleveland—and a powerful determination to further the town's development.

Tootie embarked upon this initiative two years later when she teamed up with Harvie Heitman to build a hotel that would be named in honor of her son. The 41-room Bradford Hotel opened in time for Thanksgiving in 1905. The next month it became the site of one of the biggest social events to take place in Fort Myers to that point when Tootie married her high school sweetheart, Dr. Marshall Terry.

In high school, Tootie had fallen in love with Terry, a struggling medical student and so poor he did not dare ask for her hand in marriage. After graduating from medical school, Terry moved to New York to find fame and fortune. He lifted himself from his past poverty exceedingly well, becoming the Surgeon General of the State of New York, and a Brigadier General in the Association of Military Surgeons during the Spanish-American War (where he developed new medical and surgical outfits for the National Guard and a stretcher with a mechanically adjustable pillow). But Marshall Terry had never married and still carried a torch for Tootie. After Ambrose died, he visited Fort Myers to see his old flame, now age 57. Sparks re-ignited and the two married in December 1905.

While Tootie had backed Harvie Heitman in the Bradford Hotel, she did not take part in its day-to-day operations. But the hotel business beckoned again the following year when Dr. C. Harvey Hartman of Dover, New Jersey found himself unable to reopen the nationally renowned Royal Palm Hotel in Fort Myers due to a lack of working capital resulting from a money panic that reached its crescendo in 1907. Built in 1898 by New York department store magnate Hugh O'Neill, the Royal Palm was an ultra-modern first-class winter resort that featured electric lights, a ladies' retiring and bath room with two porcelain tubs on each floor, and lush gardens containing tropical and semitropical shrubs, plants and palms, including the majestic royal palms from which the hotel eventually derived its name. To attract guests to the Royal Palm, O'Neill purchased ads in the leading newspapers in New York, Boston, Philadelphia and Washington that extolled the weather, fishing and small-town atmosphere of Fort Myers. He even hired a top-notch publicist to write stories about the celebrities and socialites who frequented his hotel. Every time one of them caught a fish or shot an alligator on a hunting trip up river, an account of the exploit was sent to their hometown newspaper. As a result, scores of publicity-seeking socialites, celebrities and business leaders flocked to the Royal Palm, which became the place to be and be seen. But O'Neill died suddenly at the age of 58 in 1902, and Hartman purchased the hotel in 1904, bought the adjoining property, built an addition, and made numerous improvements before losing his line of credit. The hotel's closing was a blow to the town and the national reputation that O'Neill had so painstakingly built.

With two large groves, numerous tracts of land throughout the county and her interest in the Bradford Hotel, Tootie had way too much at stake to allow the Royal Palm to remain boarded up. So she purchased the landmark in early 1907 and immediately constructed a 50-room addition, doubling the size and allure of the inn. After lavishly appointing both the old and new wings, she set about rectifying the most immediate problem affecting the hotel and the downtown business district at-large. The waterfront had become a malodorous eyesore strewn with rubbish and decaying hyacinths and characterized by rickety old wharves and decrepit boathouses. But Tootie was forward-thinking. Rather than merely hiring workers to clean the banks in and around the Royal Palm, she proposed that the city construct a concrete seawall 200 feet off the bank of the river and fill in the gap with sand and shell dredged up from the river bottom.

After months of public and private debate, the waterfront property owners resolved to build the seawall at their own expense.

It was actually Richard Quintus Richards, a pharmacist and owner of Royal Palm Pharmacy, who made the deal to bring Spring Training baseball to Fort Myers. In 1922, Richards established the Fort Myers Kiwanis Club. In his capacity as the chairman of the Kiwanis' baseball committee, he placed the abandoned Terry Park into service as a Major League Baseball Spring Training facility and persuaded Connie Mack to bring the Philadelphia Athletics to Fort Myers. The contract that Mack signed on January 26, 1924 was actually with the Kiwanis, and once penned, the Athletics trained at Terry Park every spring through 1936.

Starting with the Philadelphia Athletics in 1924 and ending with George Brett's Kansas City Royals in 1987, Terry Park has hosted some of the greatest teams and players in the history of Major League Baseball. Hall of Famers Jimmy Foxx, Bob Feller, Tris Speaker, Ty Cobb, Babe Ruth and Roberto Clemente are just a few of the great players that have graced the Terry Park Field. The Philadelphia Athletics were followed by the Cleveland Indians, Pittsburgh Pirates and the Kansas City Royals. Today, over 160 college baseball teams from around the country use Terry Park in the month of March to begin their college season. In 1995 the ball field was placed on the National Register of Historical Places by the United States Department of the Interior. Lee County Parks & Recreation celebrated the 100-year anniversary of Terry Park in 2006.

The project took four years to complete, but when it was done, the seawall and expanded riverfront extended from present-day Monroe all the way to Billy's Creek. But to her chagrin, Tootie could not persuade her fellow waterfront property owners to give the city a 75-foot-wide swath along the water's edge for a river walk or promenade. Lacking Tootie's aesthetic sensibility, marketing acumen and vision for the future, they could not abide giving up their private boat landings, riverfront gardens and riparian* rights no matter how picturesque a riverfront boulevard might seem.

Tootie makes an offer the city can't refuse

Even before she acquired the Royal Palm Hotel, or perhaps in contemplation of its purchase, Tootie did something else to increase the allure of Fort Myers for winter residents and out-of-town visitors. She donated 40 acres east of town for the creation of a golf and country club. It was an idea that hotelier Harvey Hartman had advanced when he bought the Royal Palm in 1904 and one that her first husband, Ambrose, had suggested as far back as 1897 when he donated an acre of land in east Fort Myers as the site for a country club.

While Ambrose and Tootie had first been attracted to the area by its fishing and weather, they quickly perceived that people, especially big earners from the northeast, needed something else to do. They needed golf, and now Marshall Terry took charge of forming the Fort Myers Yacht & Country Club. He hired the town's leading contractor, Manuel S. Gonzalez, to build "an artistic and comfortable" clubhouse and 18-hole golf course. But the club's viability was scuttled by the absence of roads to the club. The clutching sand made the club inaccessible by car and bike. By horse and buggy the trip took more than an hour each way. Members lost interest, and the course was never completed. The property was eventually converted into the Spring Training home of the Philadelphia Athletics, Cleveland Indians and Pittsburgh Pirates. While "Terry Park" is no longer used for Spring Training, it was Tootie and Marshall Terry's 40-acre donation that created the platform that subsequently made Fort Myers a perennial Grapefruit League venue and the current Spring Training home of the Boston Red Sox and the Minnesota Twins.

Spurred by the bitter lessons they learned in conjunction with the Fort Myers Yacht & Country Club, the Terrys resolved to make it easier for visitors to get into and out of Fort Myers. The roads leading in and out of town consisted of two sets of ruts cut into the sand by oxcart wheels, referred to by

*Under the riparian principle, all landowners whose property adjoins a body of water have the right to make reasonable use of it as it flows through or over their property.

locals as "Wish to God" roadways because no matter which set of ruts you chose, you always wished to God that you'd taken the other set. As a result, people either took the train or a riverboat (the Menge Brothers provided steamer service between Fort Myers and Punta Gorda via the glamorous 120-foot double-decker *St. Lucie* and her brother ship, the *Thomas A. Edison*). But for longer voyages to Tampa and Key West, deeper draft schooners were still required. These docked at the deep water wharf at the Tarpon House in Punta Rassa. But as there was only a crude unpaved trail connecting Punta Rassa to the business district downtown, passengers still had to wait around for a ride upriver on board the St. Lucie or Thomas A. Edison. So in early 1912, Tootie McGregor Terry famously offered to construct a 50-foot-wide macadam boulevard from Punta Rassa to Whiskey Creek if the city and county would complete the hard-surface road from that point to Monroe Street.

As Tootie's offer even included all necessary bridges, culverts and maintenance of the 20-mile stretch for the next five years, the city council and county commission readily agreed. Tootie had but one stipulation. She wanted the road's name changed from Riverside Drive to McGregor Boulevard in memory of Ambrose.

Tootie died a few months later before work on the roadway started, but Marshall saw to it that her promises were honored. Spurred by the roadbuilding activity that Tootie had engendered, the city went on to hard surface the shell and sand streets in town with shell asphalt (which would be replaced several years later by brick pavers, many of which were recovered and restored during the city's award-winning Streetscape program of 2004-2008).

While it would be nearly another decade before Dixie Highway and Tamiami Trail provided motorists access from Arcadia, Tampa and Miami, it was Tootie McGregor Terry who got the process started and positioned the town to participate in the Great Real Estate Boom of the mid-1920s that changed Fort Myers' look and landscape forever.

FLORIDA SHULTZ HEITMAN

A Florida Girl Through and Through

In 1894, Harvie Heitman was invited to ring in the New Year at George Shultz's Tarpon House in Punta Rassa. For 15 years, Shultz had hosted elaborate New Year's Eve dinners. Shultz had a business reason for including Heitman on the guest list that year: the 22-year-old had just opened a small general store on the corner of First and Jackson Streets. Characterized as a visionary, Harvie wasn't content to simply stock his store with groceries, tasty treats and domestic goods. He also carried high-end fishing tackle, hunting gear and camping equipment that catered to the wealthy yachtsmen who sailed upriver from the Tarpon House to fish and hunt. But Shultz got more than just a profitable business relationship that night. He got a future son-in-law as well.

Shultz's 20-year-old daughter, Florida, was at the party too. Born in Elizabeth, New Jersey, Florida Abbie Shultz grew up in Punta Rassa, where she became an avid and accomplished fisherwoman, as exemplified by a famous photograph of her posing with a tarpon weighing 185 pounds. Known to family and friends as Miss Flossie, she attended Mary's College in Burlington, New Jersey from 1889-1893 and graduated with honors.

A commuting courtship
Florida and Harvie began seeing each other after that night in spite of the two-hour boat ride from downtown Fort Myers to the

Tarpon House and the notoriously long hours that Heitman devoted to his new store, mammoth bakery and thriving livery stables.

The courtship lasted two and a half years, with Harvie finally asking George Shultz for Florida's hand during the Tarpon House's legendary Independence Day celebration in 1897. The couple exchanged vows on October 6 of that year in the dining room of Florida's grandmother in Jersey City, New Jersey.

After returning from their honeymoon, Harvie immersed himself in his store, livery, town council meetings and business travel. Besides establishing and maintaining the couple's hectic schedule and social calendar, civic-minded Florida joined Olive Stout, Flossie Hill and Julia Hanson in forming the Fort Myers Woman's Club in 1900, and was elected the organization's first vice-president.

Two years later, Florida enjoyed the unique privilege of moving into the most historic house in town. For several years, Harvie had coveted the Travers house across the street from his general store. The structure had once been the commanding officer's quarters in the old Seminole Indian and Civil War fort. It had been occupied by then Captain Winfield Scott Hancock and his wife Allie. It was where Fort Myers' first daughter, Ada Elizabeth Hancock, was born in 1857. When schooner captain Manuel A. Gonzalez arrived in February of 1866, he had converted what was left of the two-story, eight-room building into a home for himself, wife Evalina, and their children. Evalina had made the place the town's first schoolhouse when she homeschooled her own children and those of neighbor John Powell. F.A. Hendry's father and mother-in-law, Mr. and Mrs. Louis Lanier, purchased the property after the Gonzalezes moved

Florida Schultz Heitman was born in New Jersey and raised in Punta Rassa. She graduated with honors from Mary's College in Burlington, New Jersey. (Courtesy of *Fort Myers News-Press* archives.)

Growing up in Punta Rassa, Florida Schultz Heitman became an avid and accomplished fisherwoman. Here she is pictured with a 185-pound tarpon she caught. (Courtesy of Southwest Florida Museum of History.)

in 1872 to homestead 160 acres just west of town. The Laniers dealt the house to James E. Hendry, who sold it in turn to R. Ingram O. Travers. Travers spent a great deal of time and money adding rare palms and flowering plants to the shrubs and tropical fruit trees that already adorned the property, including the magnificent date palm that Captain Hancock had planted on the occasion of his daughter's birth. According to the *Fort Myers Press*, it was "the most beautiful home and surroundings" in town and "attract[ed] the attention of all who visit Fort Myers."

Harvie knew he had to work a deal to get Travers to part with the property, so he induced Tootie McGregor to sell him her half of Seminole Lodge. Heitman immediately traded the property to Travers for the much sought-after home.

Civic-minded Florida finds work-life balance

The Heitmans would hold many gatherings at their historic residence over the years, including dances, dinners, and "boisterous" euchre games. Harvie and Florida also continued to beautify the house and grounds, adding a collection of rare palms and a concrete and wrought iron fence that made the place a horticultural showcase.

In comparison to the "commodious residence and beautiful grounds," the surrounding town looked increasingly shabby. This inevitably inspired Florida to band together in 1907 with nine other women to form a Civic League for purposes of banishing free-ranging cattle from the town, and planting trees and installing park benches to beautify the streets. She also helped the League

The Heitmans held many gatherings at their historic residence over the years, including dances, dinners, and "boisterous" euchre games. (Courtesy of Southwest Florida Historical Society.)

Florida and Harvie Heitman's daughter, Lorraine, at high school graduation. (Courtesy of *The News-Press* Archives.)

raise $30,000 for research in the fight against tuberculosis, a disease from which her father suffered and that had prompted him to transfer in 1866 from the International Ocean Telegraph Co. in Newark, New Jersey to Punta Rassa.

In 1908, Florida and Harvie celebrated the birth of their only child, Lorraine. They accorded the honor of being the child's godmother to family friend and financial backer Tootie McGregor Terry. During the next seven years, Harvie did his part to clean up the town by tearing down the haphazard collection of ragtag wood structures that dotted First Street. He replaced them with handsome, state-of-the-art brick edifices that included the Bank of Fort Myers, the Earnhardt Building, the Bradford Arcade and the Evans-Heitman store on the northeast corner of First and Hendry Streets. Florida concentrated on Lorraine, her aging parents and beloved brother, along with the couple's congested social calendar and Civic League matters. During World War I, she joined forces with the Girls Junior Auxiliary of the local chapter of the American Red Cross to raise funds to buy Christmas presents for American soldiers fighting in France.

Harvie died of stomach cancer on the evening of April 17, 1922. He was only 49 years old. Not long after, Florida built a home on the corner of McGregor and Plumosa. Soon after, she moved out of the historic grand home she had shared with her husband for 20 years. A few years later, Harvie's estate moved the house to the back of the lot, intending to build a 10-story hotel on the site. However, those plans were abandoned when the Florida Real Estate Boom ended in 1927 and was followed two years later by the Great Depression. Fittingly, the library moved into the abandoned house in 1926 and made it their home for the next 12 years, when the rickety old building was condemned and torn down.

Although Florida now lived on the periphery of town, she continued to take an interest in the city to which her husband had given the last measure of his dedication and devotion. In 1927, she helped form the Caloosahatchee Chapter of the Daughters of the American Revolution, for which she served as Organizing Vice-Regent. She served on its Board of Directors and maintained an active membership until 1945. During the 1930s, she joined developer John Morgan Dean in surrendering the riparian rights she held along the riverfront to pave the way for the city to fill in a portion of the river bottom to build the Fort Myers Yacht Basin, Hall of Fifty States Civic Center and, eventually, the new library.

Florida died of a heart attack on July 5, 1945. She was 71 years old. Hers was a life in balance, with her time, attention and loving devotion divided proportionately among her husband, daughter, family and friends and the causes in which she most believed. A lesser woman would have never been able to emerge from the long shadow cast by her smart and ambitious husband. But Florida Abbie Shultz Heitman was her own person. She knew exactly who she was and what held value in her life. Fort Myers was indeed fortunate that she was part of its early history, and its culture, beauty and heritage are all the better for her efforts and involvement.

ALICE HENDRY TOOKE MCCANN

The Woman Who Helped Escort Fort Myers
into the Communications Age

Alice Hendry was one of four children born to Charles and Jane L. Hendry. During the winter of 1872-73, Charles joined his cousins, Captain F.A. and W. Marion Hendry, in driving their herds of scrub cattle to pasturelands below the Caloosahatchee River. As Charles' herds were going to graze in Glades country near the Big Cypress, he lodged Jane and the kids in a spare two-room cabin located near present-day Immokalee. But then the couple's eldest child, 6-year-old Esther Ann, got sick and died and Jane insisted on moving to Fort Myers so that she would have neighbors to help her if any of the other children were to become injured or fall ill.

Alice spent her formative years in Fort Myers, playing with her siblings, numerous cousins and the Vivas kids. During most of that time, the family lived on a large tract of riverfront property which today is bordered by Monroe Street to the west, Hendry to the east, and Second to the south. But in 1883, Charles moved to Key West in order to receive, broker and ship the cattle that the Hendrys and Dr. T.E. Langford sent him from the port in Punta Rassa. The family followed. But when Charles died ten years later, Jane immediately moved the family back to Fort Myers, building a house on the corner of First and present-day Broadway where the Franklin Shops now stand.

Over the next several years, Alice married John Judson Tooke. They had a daughter, who they named Ammie. Alice became a widow when John died, and a bride for the second time when she married J.B. McCann. But she secured her place in the annals of Fort Myers history when she became the town's first telephone switchboard operator in 1900.

Her employer was the Lee County Telephone Company. The concern was owned by Harvie Heitman's younger brother, Gilmer McCrary Heitman. Gilmer got into the phone business as a matter of happenstance. One day, he overheard several area cattlemen discussing the town's lack of phone service. Their cattle operations would be so much easier and more profitable if the town only had telephone service, they lamented.

Town's first telephone switchboard operator

Fort Myers was way behind the times. The first telephone exchange had opened in early 1878 in Hartford, Connecticut. Telephone service had promptly spread throughout the country, but not to Fort Myers. Even though it was the winter residence of Thomas Edison, Fort Myers had only got its first electrical lights two years before, in 1898, when Bertie Gardner installed a dynamo to provide power to Hugh O'Neill's newly completed Royal Palm Hotel. Heck, the town still had no rail service and the mail was still delivered and sent via the schooners and steamers that plied the Caloosahatchee and Gulf waters en route to and from Tampa and Key West. So the only way to get messages in or out of Fort Myers on a same day basis was the telegraph station in town. But that was hardly convenient for cattlemen, who had to leave their ranches and ride for hours just to send a cable, which is why the cattlemen that day were hoping that someone would start a telephone company in town one day soon.

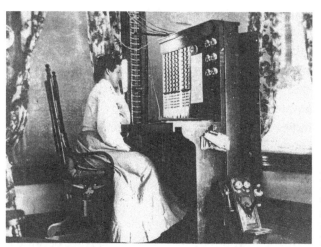

Alice Hendry Tooke McCann at the town's first switchboard, a six-circuit 50-drop exchange. (Courtesy of Southwest Florida Historical Society.)

Gilmer decided after doing some research that he would be that some-one. He had saved a small amount of money and it was just enough to cover the cost of the equipment he would need to purchase and install a telephone exchange. He undoubtedly sought the advice of his brother, Harvie, who had quite a head for business himself. Harvie invited Gilmer to set up the exchange on the second floor of the brand new brick building he'd erected on the north-west corner of Jackson and First thanks to financing by Standard Oil executive Ambrose McGregor.

With everything in place, Gilmer applied to the county commission for a franchise to provide phone service throughout Lee County (which included Collier and Hendry counties at the time). The franchise granted, the Lee County Telephone Company opened for business on February 21, 1900 with Alice Hendry Tooke McCann sitting behind the company's six-circuit 50-drop exchange.

Before the advent of automatic exchanges, an operator was needed for anything other than calling telephones across a shared party line. When the caller lifted the receiver and cranked the generator in the phone housing, a light would come on over the jack for that phone in the switchboard at the phone company's central office. The switchboard operator then inserted a plug into the jack, asked who the caller wished to speak to, and completed the circuit by inserting a second plug into the appropriate jack for the other phone. Being in complete control of the call, the operator was in the position to listen to private con-versations, and Alice admitted to listening in to the calls that passed through her exchange. In fact, when the Lee County Telephone Co. added Sunday service in 1903, she confessed to being entertained by courting lovers making dates for Sunday evenings who there-after spooned on the phone for hours.

Alice may have heard about the great fire of 1903 from a pan-icked caller on the morning of October 16, or she may have just

Alice Hendry Tooke McCann may have been Fort Myers' first telephone switchboard operator, but Emma Nutt was the nation's first female telephone operator. She went to work on September 1, 1878 for the Boston Telephone Dispatch Company. Early on, phone companies commonly employed women as phone operators for a variety of reasons. The companies claimed that women were more courteous, but in reality, women represented cheap labor. They commanded between half and a quarter of what the phone companies had to pay male operators. Moreover, by filling these positions with young, attractive single "girls next door," their public relations and marketing departments were able to exploit their gender and looks to promote their telephone service. No information has been found regarding the amount Gilmer Heitman paid Alice McCann or how her pay compared to what male operators may have received either locally or elsewhere in Florida.

smelled the smoke. The wind was carrying dense smoke and burning embers toward the Heitman brick building that day from the source of the fire in the Roberts building up on Oak (Main) and Hendry. It's likely that Alice abandoned her post when the second alarm was sounded, beckoning every able bodied man, woman and child to form a bucket brigade after a valve stuck, disabling the town's only fire pump. History recounts that Alice was among the women who stepped forward when Flossie Hill rallied her friends to take over for the spent volunteers after they'd got the fire pump working again just in the nick of time.

And so it was that Alice Hendry Tooke McCann had a hand in saving the town from total destruction that day–although historians like Karl Grismer credited a nearby crew of railroad line construction workers with putting out the blaze. However that may be, there is no denying that Alice helped escort the town into the communications age as the town's first telephone switchboard operator.

ELLA MAE PIPER

Business Legend and Pillar of the Community

Ella Mae Bailor was born into poverty in 1884 in southern Georgia, the only daughter of Ned Bailor and Sarah Williams. Ella came to Fort Myers as a teenager when her mother moved here. There were no schools for blacks in Fort Myers at that time but somehow Ella got schooling, either in Georgia before the move or privately in Fort Myers after the move. Her mother found work as a domestic servant and also married again. Ella took her new stepfather's last name of Jones.

Ella left a short time later to attend Atlanta's Spelman College, a school for black women, but there is no record of her graduating. It is unknown what Ella did during her 20s—perhaps she was just trying to earn a living—but we do know that in 1915 she graduated from the renowned Rohrer Institute of Beauty Culture in New York City. Upon graduation she worked as a hairdresser and masseuse at New York's upscale Twilight Inn.

In 1916 Ella returned to Fort Myers, presumably to be near her mother, who was working as a domestic employee in the home of banker/hotel owner/real estate developer Harvie Heitman. When Ella moved back to town, she established the Fort Myers Beauty Salon—the town's first—on the outskirts of Safety Hill. She later moved the salon from Jackson Street to a location on Hendry for a short time before finally relocating the shop to 1819 Evans, where she could work closer to home.

Uses business acumen to overcome race and gender discrimination
For the business to survive, Ella had to draw affluent customers. Whether it was her experience having worked with wealthy customers in New York City, or her skill as a beautician, or her elegant and fashionable bearing, she did indeed attract such a clientele. Her salon was tastefully furnished and was said to be "airy and cool, not cramped." In fact, the business did so well that Ella hired an assistant, a young girl named Anna Heard. Ella sent Anna to beauty college and then turned over the shop's daily operations to her. This freed Ella to concentrate on her chiropody. As with today's podiatrists, treatment of the hands and feet included caring for skin and nail conditions, something Ella apparently was so gifted at, she was requested to make house calls to the town's most influential residents. Besides providing soothing body and foot treatments, Ella's skill with difficult cases prompted her clients to affectionately call her "doctor," and "Dr." usually precedes her name to this day.

Among her regular clients were Clara Ford and Mina Edison, with whom she became close friends. Thomas Edison often accompanied his wife to the salon, which resulted in an occasional mention of Ella's salon in the *Fort Myers Press*, which rarely reported on black residents.

Ella kept her knowledge of hairstyles and beauty techniques current by regularly traveling to the big cities up north. On one such trip in December 1920, she returned to Fort Myers with a husband, Frank S. Piper. In 1925 they purchased property on Evans Avenue for her business. However, in the 1920s, married women were not allowed to own or manage their own busi-

Ella Mae Piper opened the town's first beauty salon after returning to Fort Myers in 1916. (Courtesy of Lee County Black History Society.)

Ella Mae Piper was known as a woman of grace and elegance, an independent spirit and powerful presence. (Courtesy of the artist, Cindy Jane.)

nesses without their husbands' approval. Independent-minded Ella bristled at the thought of needing her husband's approval to manage her business. She petitioned the state for permission to buy and sell property and conduct business independently, and, remarkably, the state granted her request. Her marriage, already strained from the demands and success of her business, dissolved after this.

Ever the entrepreneur, Ella established another business enterprise during the booming '20s. With a group of investors, she formed the Big Four Bottling Company, a soft drink bottling company. The plant was located on her Mango Street* and Evans Avenue property. This business, too, was a great success and afforded Ella a very comfortable lifestyle. She traveled widely and spent most summers in New York.

One of the most influential women in Florida

When Sarah Williams died in 1926, Ella assumed her mother's role in putting on an annual Christmas party for needy children in Safety Hill. By then, the yearly event had grown from the initial 1915 gathering of 15 little girls to a crowd of more than 600 girls and boys. Because of Ella's stature in the community, many churches, businesses and community leaders—black and white—pitched in and contributed gifts and donations for the youngsters. The annual Christmas party continues to this day and will celebrate its centennial in 2015.

Mango Street was renamed Dr. Ella Piper Way in 2010.

1915 Sarah Williams photo in front of her home. (Courtesy of Southwest Florida Historical Society.)

Over time, Ella became a respected community activist, philanthropist and founding member of Safety Hill. Back then, white people claimed that Safety Hill took its name from the fact that the ground was high enough to be safe from flooding during hurricanes and summer thunderstorms. But the people living in Safety Hill knew that the subdivision was the only place blacks could feel safe during the days of racial segregation. But it wasn't always that way.

Prior to 1900, blacks and whites had lived together. In fact, Fort Myers' first black settler, Nelson Tillis, married a white woman and their ten children played in the yard of newcomer Thomas Edison. But many of the people who moved into Fort Myers in the years following the turn of the 20th century were far less racially tolerant and even imposed "Jim Crow" laws that made it a crime for "people of color" to cross the railroad tracks after dark. Tillis couldn't abide the growing racial tensions and left for the Bahamas, never to be seen again. But Ella resolved to make Safety Hill and its residents the best they could be.

A firm believer in education, Ella contributed financially to Williams Academy, the first government-funded school for blacks, built in 1913. When it opened, however, it was so underfunded by the county that the school's textbooks were hand-me-downs from white schools and typically had miss-ing pages, some even missing whole sections of a subject. Today the building houses the Williams Academy Black History Museum.

Ella also helped to finance the construction of Dunbar Community School in 1927 so that black children from Lee, Charlotte and Collier County could get a high school education, something that was not possible prior to the school's opening. In addition, she was instrumental in helping young people obtain scholarships to attend Tuskegee College, sometimes using her personal funds for this purpose. As a mentor, she coached the children in oration and took many around the state to attend meetings and conferences.

She helped fund the Jones-Walker Hospital, the area's first hospital for non-whites, and helped establish a black chapter of the American Red Cross. She founded a chapter of the Daughters of Elks, an auxiliary body to the Brothers of Elks, which was begun in 1898 as an Elks organization for people of color. The Daughters of Elks, committed to community service and men-toring youth, was organized in 1902 and the Florida chapter in 1925. Her personal philanthropy included giving food and clothing to needy neigh-bors, providing housing to Negro League baseball players who were denied accommodations at area hotels, and giving assistance to the handicapped and underprivileged elderly.

Independent spirit shines through difficult times

The Great Depression affected everyone and especially families who were already struggling, such as those in Safety Hill. Both of Ella's businesses suffered and she, too, struggled to continue her philanthropic efforts. Perhaps inspired by Ella's determination and thinking outside the box, some residents of the Safety Hill neighborhood rallied together and applied to one of President Roosevelt's New Deal Programs. The group met with success when the newly formed Work Projects Administrations (WPA) funded the city's first public black high school, Dunbar High.

As head of the Fruit Flower and Plant Guild, Mina Edison supported the new high school by selecting it as a service project and the Guild provided landscaping. When Ella helped to dedicate the new school in 1937, Mina was on stage with her, a most unusual pairing in those times, when mixing of the races was usually not acceptable.

In the 1940s Safety Hill morphed into Dunbar, deriving its name from the high school that was named in honor of renowned black poet, author and playwright Paul Lawrence Dunbar.

In 1944, Ella married Cleon Harvey, a man half her age, but that marriage lasted even less time than her first, and she threw herself back into her charitable work. She sponsored musical events, some of which were held at Mount Olive African Methodist Episcopal (A.M.E.) Church, where she was a founding member. Both blacks and whites attended the performances of the black entertainers—some nationally famous—that Ella recruited.

When Ella Mae Piper died in 1954 at age 69, she followed the lead of her good friend Mina Edison and willed her home to the City of Fort Myers for "the benefit of the children, the poor and the elderly in the black community." It took the City of Fort Myers 22 years to take full advantage of the gift, but in June of 1976, the Dr. Ella Piper Center for Social Services was dedicated. Today, the Center sponsors a foster grandparent program, a senior companion program and a senior employment program, as well as various special events.

MORE
NOTABLE WOMEN

MARION TWIGGS MYERS

The Girl who Inspired the Name "Fort Myers"

Marion Isabelle Twiggs was the daughter of Major General David Emmanuel Twiggs. The General commanded federal forces in Texas from 1846-1847 during the Mexican-American War. Colonel Abraham C. Myers served under him, which is how the General's beautiful young daughter met her future husband. According to historian Karl Grismer, "[Myers'] dashing manner and merry smile won her heart," and the two embarked upon a romance in spite of the fact that the Colonel was Marion's senior by some 26 years.

When Twiggs was transferred to Fort Brooke on the west coast of Florida, Myers followed and continued his relationship with Marion. By the time General Twiggs received a directive from the War Department to establish a fort deep in Seminole Indian territory south of the Peace River, Marion and Abraham were engaged. So when the General dispatched two companies of Artillery on Valentine's Day, 1850 to set up the outpost, he mandated that the post be called Fort Myers "to honor his prospective son-in-law and please his daughter."

At Fort Brooke, Colonel Myers functioned as chief quartermaster for the entire Department of Florida. In this capacity, it was his purview to approve all architectural plans and requisition the building materials and supplies needed to build his namesake. However, neither Colonel Myers nor his wife ever visited the grand fort that bore his name.

Fort Myers was built with the express purpose of serving as a base of operations for locating, rounding up and deporting the last of the Seminole Indians still living in the Big Cypress and Everglades in the 1850s. Failing to persuade Chief Billy Bowlegs and his people to leave voluntarily, the soldiers at the fort instigated a war. When that war ended on May 4, 1858 with the involuntary deportation of Bowlegs and his tribe to Indian territory in Oklahoma, Colonel Myers was re-assigned to Washington, where Marion quickly became the belle of the nation's capital.

In *Belles, Beaux and Brains of the 60's*, author Thomas Cooper De Leon provides an illuminating account of Marion Twiggs Myers in the months preceding the start of the Civil War. "In all the mad rush that pre-bellum winter in Washington, 1860-1861, when grave heads shook ominously and light heels danced over a powder magazine and recked little when the fuse might reach, one handsome woman was constantly in evidence," De Leon wrote near the turn of the 20th century. "Colonel A.C. Myers, of the quartermaster-general's department, had married the brilliant and picturesque daughter of old General David E. Twiggs, of Mexican War fame. Grave and reticent as he was polished and accomplished, the husband was much older than his wife. [Myers] had as perfect a contempt for what he called society as his wife held delight in it… her dancing was perfect, her tact equal to it and her beauty even more exceptional."

However, Marion's days as a Washington socialite ended when Colonel Myers resigned his commission in the United States Army following the start

Marion Twiggs Myers was known for her brilliance and beauty. (Courtesy of Southwest Florida Museum of History.)

Marion Twiggs Myers in middle-age. (Courtesy of Southwest Florida Historical Society.)

of the war. He was appointed quartermaster general of the Confederate States Army in February of 1862. "Very valuable service he rendered, too, and the regular uniform adopted by the War Department was, in larger part, of his design," wrote De Leon.

Myers' larger responsibility as quartermaster general was to keep the Confederate army properly clothed and shod. Toward this end, he had at his disposal the Confederate Army's largest supply bureau, complete with 88 clerks, quartermasters in each state, paymasters and quartermasters in the field, manufacturing plants, purchasing agents abroad, and depot and post quarter-masters. But because of the South's lack of factories and manufacturing plants coupled with the Union's naval blockade, Myers was not able to obtain the clothing, shoes and other items that were needed by a top-notch fighting force. Further, he was deprived of the leather he needed for shoes by the Ordinance Department, which inexplicably felt that leather cartridge boxes and harnesses for horses pulling artillery were more important than properly shod troops. Nevertheless, it was Myers who took the brunt of growing complaints, which included the accusation that the South's defeat at Gettysburg was attributable in large measure to the pervasive lack of appropriate footwear.

Marion was not present during the initial months of her husband's tenure as the Confederate Army's Quartermaster General. Soon after his appointment, Marion departed Richmond for Europe, where "her grace and beauty made the same impression as they had done in the older capital." But Marion eventually returned to war-ravaged Virginia, where she improvidently developed an unsavory rivalry with President Jefferson Davis' wife, Varina.

According to several accounts, Marion ostensibly said at a social gathering that Varina Davis looked like "an old squaw." Apparently the war had eroded Marion's former reputation for tact and social grace because she was described during this time as sharp tongued and opinionated. Regardless, the comment was only one unfortunate volley in a long war between these leading ladies of Richmond, and given the fact that Varina Davis had a dark complexion and a generous silhouette, the remark was oft repeated, not forgotten and never forgiven.

It also didn't help that Abraham Myers was the great-grandson of Charleston's first rabbi, a descendant of an old Jewish family that settled in South Carolina generations before the war. More than 10,000 Jews fought for the Confederacy and Robert E. Lee allowed his Jewish soldiers to observe all holy days, but this did not spare Myers from suggestions that he enriched himself with his office, owing his first loyalty to "the party of Moses" and "the tribe of Levi." Marion herself, in fact, was said to be from "the Lost Tribe" of Israel.

Blamed for losses on the battlefield and losing the war in the parlors of Richmond as well, Abraham Myers was replaced as Quartermaster General on August 10, 1863. Humiliated by his termination, Myers and Marion retreated to Georgia until the end of the war. They then relocated to Weisbaden, Germany, where they lived until 1876.

Marion outlived her husband by just four years. She passed away in 1893. One of their sons, John Twiggs Myers, became a Lieutenant General and earned a place in Marine Corps history as commander of the American Legation Guard at Peking, China during the Boxer Rebellion. Interestingly, neither he nor his brother ever visited the city that today bears their name.

ADA ELIZABETH HANCOCK

Fort Myers' First Daughter

Ada Elizabeth Hancock was the first non-Native American baby born in Fort Myers. She was born in 1857 to Captain Winfield Scott Hancock and his wife, Almira, inside the commanding officer's quarters on the site of what is now the Sidney & Berne Davis Art Center.

Growing up, Ada loved to read and her father showered her with the finest literature of the day. He also commissioned a celebrated artist by the name of B.F. Reinhart to paint her portrait. The painting depicts a soft, sensitive-looking girl with clear, clean features, large blue eyes, a high forehead, and tresses that reached her waist. So full of promise, Ada died of typhoid fever on March 28, 1875. She was barely 19.

In *Hancock the Superb*, author Glenn Tucker reports that "no other loss had ever struck the general such a blow."

Regrettably, Hancock was no stranger to loss. From Pennsylvania, Hancock fought on the side of the Union during the Civil War. Credited with defeating Robert E. Lee at Gettysburg, he was defending the middle line when Pickett made his immortal charge. In the heat of battle, Hancock's dearest friend, Confederate General Lewis Armistead, was fatally shot as he led his men into Hancock's lines. Hancock also lost a close election for president in 1880, barely losing to James A. Garfield by 7,000 votes.

General Hancock and his wife returned to Fort Myers several times between Ada's death and the General's own demise in 1886. Legend has it that on the day Ada was born, then Captain Hancock planted a date seed in front of the officer's quarters. The seed sprouted and grew into a tall and magnificent date palm. Captain Manuel Gonzalez tended to the tree after he moved his family into the commanding officer's quarters in 1866, as did Mr. and Mrs. Louis Lanier, who purchased the property in 1873 after the Gonzalezes moved out of the town center.

Almira and General Hancock made periodic pilgrimages to see the date palm because it reminded them of their daughter. Over time, the tree became one of Fort Myers' most beloved and famous landmarks. The town nearly lost the tree during a hurricane in 1910, but new owners Harvie and Florida Heitman were able to prop up and brace the palm. Unfortunately, the tree was so badly damaged by the hurricane of October 22, 1921 that it had to be destroyed. Over the succeeding years, the tree and the girl for whom it was planted faded from memory. But today, the people of Fort Myers remember Ada Elizabeth Hancock as the town's first daughter.

Fort Myers' "First Daughter" Ada Hancock. (Courtesy of Southwest Florida Historical Society.)

MARY VERDIER PARKER

Fort Myers' First Paid Female Teacher

From its inception, Fort Myers placed a heavy emphasis on education. Original settler Evalina Weatherford Gonzalez homeschooled her own children and those of neighbor John Powell. After the Gonzalezes moved west of the fort and the Hendrys took their place within the confines of the old fort a year later, F.A. Hendry persuaded Englishman Robert Bell (see more on Robert Bell in Sidebar, p. 92) to teach his and the other children living in the tiny settlement.

Back then, Southwest Florida was part of Monroe County, and in 1878, the county finally opened a school in Fort Myers. The county hired Howell Parker to serve as principal and as the school's first teacher as well. But the ensuing spring, Howell went into business with general store owner Jehu Blount. In order to get more foot traffic into their Parker-Blount General Store, Jehu pulled some political strings and got Howell appointed the town's second postmaster in August 1879. With his time now at a premium, Howell decided he needed a replacement and so he brought in a new schoolteacher that fall. Her name was Mary Verdier and she was from Beaufort, South Carolina.

Mary was as pretty as she was intelligent. A widower with an 8-year-old daughter, Parker fell hard for the new teacher, and the couple married the following March.

"The wedding was a grand event," relates historian Karl Grismer. "Cattlemen, hunters, merchants and boatmen put on their best Sunday-go-to-meeting clothes and the women their starched muslins and crinolines. The bride, dressed in snowy white, was attended by her older girl pupils who served as bridesmaids." But the wedding marked the end of Mary's tenure as teacher.

After returning from their honeymoon in Tampa, Mary went to work organizing the Nickel Club, an organization that raised funds for various churches and causes. Under her management, the Club raised the money to buy the town's first church organ. By the late 1880s, the organization had 29 members and began raising funds for a reading room—although it took Olive Stout, Julia Hanson and the Fort Myers Woman's Club to finally get the job done in 1903.

In the years following their nuptials, Mary settled in to running the Parker household and Howell became one of the town's leading citizens. He served on the committee that voted to incorporate Fort Myers in 1885. He was also elected the town's first mayor by a wide margin. The Parker-Blount Grocery Store thrived. After taking a year off, he was elected mayor once more. He opened his own grocery store, eventually expanding it until it became the largest commercial business in town. Howell also ventured into banking, real estate and the phosphate business, investing heavily with a number of other town leaders in a pebble phosphate mining operation. The latter proved improvident. The company folded during the great money panic of 1893. Howell lost everything and was forced to declare bankruptcy. Although others also lost their fortunes, including Marion Hendry, Howell could not handle the embarrassment and he and Mary left town for good.

Mary Verdier Parker never made it back to Fort Myers. She died in Bartow, Florida on May 21, 1900. Her obituary described her as "a woman of fine character; her loyalty and devotion to the church were above praise."

Although Robert Bell loved literature and knew virtually all of Shakespeare's plays by rote, he knew nothing about frontier life or even how to ride a horse. F.A. Hendry offered Bell a salary of $25 per month, free room and board, all the fishing and hunting he wanted, horseback riding lessons, and the use of Hendry's best sorrel pony all winter long. It was an offer Bell could not refuse, and his first class in the little log cabin that the county provided included ten children: Virginia Lee, George and Frank Hendry, Ida and Mattie Blount, Amelia Vivas, James Hendry (son of Charles and Jane L. Hendry), and Lavenia, Mary and Manuel Gonzalez.

In October of 1888, Howell Parker's great-nephew came to live with Howell and Mary and learn the grocery store business. He stayed on after Howell and Mary left town, and during the next 29 years, he would go on to become the town's most successful business owner, commercial builder and banker. His name was Harvie E. Heitman.

MARY PERRY LAYCOCK

"Fairy Godmother" of the Fort Myers Library

Mary Perry Laycock came to Fort Myers in 1903 with her son, Harry, who had come to town to sell electrical equipment to the Seminole Power & Ice Co. When Harry decided to stay on and serve as the company's plant manager, Mary, a widow, decided to make Fort Myers home, too.

Almost immediately, Mary became active as a church worker, first with the Methodist Church and later with the Presbyterian Church, of which she was a charter member. But Mary's true passion was children and books, and over the next two decades, she laid the groundwork for the Fort Myers library.

The library had its origins in a reading room set up by the Fort Myers Woman's Club. Upon its opening, Mary worked tirelessly with its president, Julia Hanson, to secure donations of books, magazines, and newspapers from locals and winter residents. She went on from there to raise the funds necessary to keep the reading room running, chairing the Funds Solicitation Committee, a post she executed with vigor and grace from 1905 until 1926. Subscribers paid the librarian's salary of $1 per week and the rent, for a total of $12.71 per month. Tootie McGregor Terry was among the major donors. Librarians served on a rotating basis, and Mary took turns along with Olive Stout and Julia Hanson.

According to local historian Karl Grismer, it was largely because of Laycock's untiring work that the reading room was maintained, enlarged and finally culminated in the library that found its home in 1926 in the former historic home of Harvie and Florida Heitman. For her efforts, Mary earned the affectionate title of the "Fairy Godmother of the Fort Myers Library."

Mary died in 1931 at the age of 80.

Mary Laycock. (Courtesy of Southwest Florida Historical Society.)

The former historic home of Harvie and Florida Heitman housed the Fort Myers Library from 1926 until 1938. (Courtesy of Southwest Florida Historical Society.)

JULIA ISABEL FRIERSON HENDRY

The Woman Who Ushered Fort Myers into the Modern Era

A year after the Hendrys and Blounts joined Joe and Christiana Vivas in Fort Myers, a former major in the Confederate Army by the name of Aaron Frierson heard about the nascent cow town on the Caloosahatchee while living in Tampa. Frierson took a boat ride down the coast to check out the town. It was smaller than he had expected, but Frierson decided its prospects looked good, so he moved his family. Soon after, he went into business with Marion Hendry, opening a general store under the name of Frierson & Hendry on the northeast corner of First and Hendry.

Frierson and his wife, Mary, had three children: Taylor, Ella and Julia. It is not likely that Julia was happy about the move. She had just been crowned Miss Tampa a few months before. But by the end of the year, Julia had met and become engaged to one of Marion Hendry's nephews, James E. Hendry, the son of F.A. and Ardeline Hendry. Jimmy was following in his dad's footsteps, working in the cattle business.

The couple set a wedding date of June 14, 1875, but the day of the wedding came and went and there was no sign of Jimmy. Julia kept her wedding dress and trousseau at the ready, but the next day still no Jimmy. Keeping the faith, she refreshed the church flowers and was rewarded on the third day with her betrothed's arrival. Jimmy had been working on the frontier and couldn't get back to

Fort Myers—or even get word to Julia—because of severe weather out on the range. They were married on June 17.

Julia and James were not Fort Myers' first bride and groom. That honor went the year before to Jimmy's sister, Laura, and telegraph operator Waddy Thompson. But Julia and James helped settle the town, and it was the former Miss Tampa who drove the last spike in the railroad ties that brought the Atlantic Coast Line Railroad to Fort Myers on February 20, 1904, propelling the former cow town into the modern era.

According to historian Karl Grismer, Fort Myers celebrated the railroad's arrival in a big way. The last rail went down at 11 a.m. at Monroe Street, where Atlantic Coast Line was building its railroad dock. "The large town flag was secured and Engine No. 499 was draped in the national colors," the *Fort Myers Press* reported at the time. "Then young ladies hustled about and secured large bunches of flowers and soon had the headlight, flag standards and pilot of the engine bedecked with flowers. Mrs. Frierson and Mrs. James E. Hendry sent an immense and beautiful bouquet to F.L. Long and the other railroad men.

"Our people practically took control of the train as the work neared completion. Mrs. J.E. Foxworthy and Misses Dot Stout and Bessie Thorpe held up the engineer. M.E. Moye took charge of the bell rope and whistle cord and kept the bell and whistle going. Colonel E.L. Evans fired a salute with his brass cannon. Shortly after 11 a.m., the last rail slid from the flat car and was thrown into place.

Julia Isabel Frierson Hendry, a former Miss Tampa, kept the faith for three days when her groom was caught out on the range in severe weather with no way to let her know. (Courtesy of Larry Wiggins.)

An older Julia Hendry. (Courtesy of Southwest Florida Historical Society.)

"Then, as the last spike was made ready, Mrs. James E. Hendry was escorted to the track, given a sledgehammer, and drove home the last spike that held the rails that connected Fort Myers with the great railroad system of the Atlantic Coast Line Railroad and the entire country.

"Then the crowd cheered, the cannon boomed, whistles blew and bells rang ... and all hands clambered on the engine, tender and flat cars and were given the first ride over the new railroad through Fort Myers and out to the county road crossing two miles east of the courthouse. Many on the train had never ridden on a railroad, so the affair proved a proud and joyful event."

Serving as the veritable center of attention during the height of the festivities, Julia Isabel Frierson Hendry thus secured her place in the annals of Fort Myers history.

CLOSE CONNECTIONS

James and Julia's son, James E. Hendry, Jr., married Olive and Frank Stout's daughter, Florence. Always interested in horticulture, James, Jr. started a nursery in 1908 that grew into the Everglades Nursery, which was, at the time, one of the largest of its kind anywhere in the world. One of James, Jr.'s employees at the nursery was a young girl named Helen, whose contributions as a notable woman are recounted later in this book. Sharing a deep sense of mutual admiration, James, Jr. hybridized a rare thornless bougainvillea for her, and she propagated and named a yellow hibiscus for him. Helen married James, Jr.'s son, James E. Hendry III in 1969, and together they ran the nursery until 1987.

Barbara B. Mann

Champion of the Arts

Barbara Kingsbury Balch, or "B" as everyone called her, spent her early years in Topfield, Massachusetts. In 1923 her divorced mother moved 10-year-old Barbara and her sister, Helen, to Fort Myers to live with the girls' maternal grandparents. Barbara and Helen sang duets and performed for Connie Mack and the Philadelphia Athletics their first year in town as part of a successful effort to lure the team to Fort Myers for Spring Training. Six years later Barbara graduated from Fort Myers High School, receiving her diploma from Thomas Edison himself.

Barbara met George T. Mann in 1935 while they were both playing the leads in an amateur performance at the Pleasure Pier in downtown Fort Myers. They married in 1938 and in 1947 they founded George T. Mann Construction. George served as general contractor and Barbara as office manager and bookkeeper. A talented pianist and singer, Barbara also served as a church organist and choir director at various churches, and spent 30 years at First Presbyterian Church, retiring from her church career in 1998 at age 85.

Barbara was instrumental in the founding of almost every arts organization in the county. She served as the charter president of the Alliance for the Arts in Fort Myers, which, as the state-designated local agency, supports individual artists and arts organizations throughout Lee County. In addition to the Alliance, Barbara was a founding director in 1948 of the Fort Myers Community Concert Association, and served as the organization's president for 57 years. She also founded the community chorus, the Edison Choraliers, and helped found the Southwest Florida Symphony. She served as president of the Fort Myers Woman's Community Club and the Rotary-Anns, an early spin-off of Rotary International for wives of Rotary members.*

"She was so energetic," said son Frank Mann in an interview with NBC in December 2013. "I just never saw her rest. She never took a nap. When she got up in the morning, it was full speed ahead. You better get out of the way or be going with her."

Barbara was known to be gracious and charming and a strong-willed person you didn't say 'no' to; hence, everybody wanted her on their arts committees or in their clubs! As a result, Barbara B. Mann's name is synonymous with arts and culture in Lee County and throughout Southwest Florida. Today, her legacy is perpetuated by the Lee County Alliance for the Arts and the Barbara B. Mann Performing Arts Hall. She and her son Frank, a former state representative and state senator and now a Lee County Commissioner, spearheaded efforts to build the 1,800-seat performance center in south Fort Myers, which was the first of its kind in Southwest Florida. As a tribute to Barbara's inspired decades of leadership in the arts and culture of Southwest Florida, the Florida Legislature named the new performing arts hall at Edison College after her.

Barbara was devoted to her husband, George, and their two highly respected sons. "Barbara's love of family, passion for sharing arts and culture with all who can be touched, and her humble appreciation of those around her offer just a glimpse of her tremendous female spirit," wrote Deirdre Mann in honoring Barbara as a Rotary-Ann Angel. "We learn from Barbara to maintain a strong sense of self and how women are best served lifting one another up."

Barbara had always dreamed of going to college, but it was not possible for a young woman growing up during the depression. In her sixties, she enrolled at Edison Community College and earned a two-year degree, then earned a bachelor's degree at the Thomas Edison State College of New Jersey.

*One of the world's first service organizations, Rotary International was founded by Chicagoan Paul Harris in 1905. After decades of unsuccessful efforts by men and women all over the world to allow for the admission of women into Rotary clubs, in 1987 the U.S. Supreme Court ruled that Rotary Clubs may not exclude women from membership. In 1989, at its first meeting after the Supreme Court decision, the Rotary Council on Legislation voted to eliminate the requirement in its Constitution that membership be limited to men. After that, women were welcomed into Rotary clubs around the world.

Barbara died in 2013 at the age of 100, just three weeks shy of her 101st birthday.

Understanding that the arts is not only an economic engine, but also a key ingredient for quality of life, Barbara became *the* pioneer of performing arts in Southwest Florida. (Courtesy of *The News-Press* Archives.)

Pleasure Pier in downtown Fort Myers, where Barbara Balch met her future husband, George T. Mann. (Courtesy of Southwest Florida Museum of History.)

Barbara and George T. Mann with babies George Jr. and Franklin in 1937. (Courtesy of *The News-Press* Archives.)

MELISSA JONES AND CANDIS WALKER

Raised First Hospital for Non-Whites

Running pie and cake sales at churches and schools and other community gatherings, Melissa Jones and Candis Walker raised monies that were matched by other resources to build the first hospital to serve the black community of Lee County. The hospital was actually designated for blacks, Indians, and other non-whites and it was dedicated in the spring of 1924. The two-story, wooden structure on High Street served the community until the mid-1940s, when a second more modern concrete building was built at a different location.

Jones-Walker Hospital had one black doctor, E.E. Velasco, who got occasional help from another black doctor from Arcadia. White doctors from Lee Memorial would take shifts at Jones-Walker when no black doctor was available. When black patients needed surgery or X-rays, they were taken to Lee Memorial, then sent right back to Jones-Walker because no black patients were allowed to stay at Lee Memorial. Dr. Velasco's brother-in-law, Gloster Allen Price (brother of Velasco's wife, Lela Price Velasco, a local school-teacher), was another black doctor in town, but he was a dentist.

Jones-Walker Hospital was closed in 1966 by court order, two years after passage of the Civil Rights Act of 1964. All patients, white and non-white, then began to be treated at Lee Memorial.

Around 1970, a housing project was built on the site and was named the Jones Walker Garden Apartments. The apartment complex remains to this day.

Candis Walker, who had two daughters, was an active civic worker in the heart of the Dunbar community, and was one of nine founders of the Fort Myers Mount Olive African Methodist Episcopal (A.M.E.) Church built in 1926. The founding group had its first organizational meeting in 1895 in the Lee County Courthouse. The group continued to operate in the downtown area wherever they could borrow meeting space. When enough money was raised, they built their own structure at Hough Street and Anderson Avenue, but had to rebuild when the hurricane of 1926 destroyed the building. Additionally, Candis organized the Candis Walker Missionary Society at Mount Olive.

Melissa Jones was active in the black chapter of the National Woman's Christian Temperance Union (WCTU), which was founded in 1874 in Ohio and quickly spread throughout the country, becoming the largest woman's organization in the U.S. The initial crusade against alcohol was a protest by women, in part, because of their lack of civil rights. The movement gradually expanded to include reform in other areas such as domestic violence, women's suffrage, owning property, and "age of consent," as leaders came to understand that all reform and social problems are interconnected. Today the WCTU is the oldest voluntary, non-sectarian woman's organization in continuous existence in the world, and it supports a wide range of programs for women and girls.

(From left to right) Artension Wilson, Melissa Jones and Candis Walker in front of the new Jones-Walker Hospital. (Courtesy of Lee County Black History Society.)

VERONICA SHOEMAKER

First African American Elected to City Council

Veronica Sapp Shoemaker was the first African American to serve on the Fort Myers City Council. She won the seat in 1982 and held it for 26 years. During that span, Veronica was active in the Lee County National Association for the Advancement of Colored People (NAACP), Lee County Leadership Council, Women in Municipal Government, Lee County AIDS Task Force, Lee County School Board Desegregation Task Force, Lee County Food Bank, Dunbar Improvement Association and National Federation of Florists. She brought resolve, determination and passion to each of these organizations. Her contributions and many diverse accomplishments are remarkable in their own right, but all the more astonishing given her humble origins.

The second of 11 children, Veronica was born in 1928 in the Dunbar community, known at that time as Safety Hill, in the deeply segregated state of Florida. Her dad was a preacher, and she grew up in a home on a dirt road that her dad had built by hand from rough-cut Florida pine. The family grew much of their own food, raising collard greens, turnips and mustard as well as cultivating fruit trees such as orange, Key Lime, avocado, guava and Japanese plum.

It's all about education

Local high schools were still segregated in the 1940s, and her awareness of the magnitude of racial inequality grew through reading, studying and learning. Grateful for the mentoring she received from her high school English teacher, Jenna Lee Kelly, Veronica used her experiences at Dunbar High to establish herself as a community leader and spokesperson. At Kelly's urging, Veronica enthusiastically accepted all the opportunities presented to her to speak at black leadership conferences and conventions.

By the time she graduated, Veronica was already setting up PTAs, the Dunbar Little League, and other organizations to better the community. After high school she accepted appointments to boards she felt provided her with a platform from which to make a difference. "It was always important to me to fulfill my vision and be involved," Veronica told *Florida Weekly* in 2007. "I prepared myself by reading a lot, studying the laws and saying yes when I was asked to serve on committees."

Given this background, she was poised to act when the United States Supreme Court handed down its decision in Brown vs. Board of Education in 1954, ruling in favor of school desegregation. Wanting African American parents to have a voice in their children's education, she took up the fight to desegregate Lee County schools. Even though it was now federal law, Florida lawmakers were in no hurry to change their ways; Lee County even less so. For 10 years the Lee County School Board refused to comply with the federal mandate, although many school boards throughout Florida had integrated their school systems. Finally, after passage of the Civil Rights Act of 1964, the Board approved a "gradual integration" plan that would take up to 12 years; however, it did not allow for integration of teachers or for transporting black

Veronica Shoemaker was a reformer and game changer in the 1960s who played a key role in bringing about the integration of Fort Myers' schools. (Courtesy of Lee County Black History Society.)

Veronica Shoemaker at age 79, standing on the railroad tracks that separated the black and white communities in Fort Myers. (Courtesy of *Naples Daily News*.)

students to white school zones. This is when Veronica, now President of the Lee County NAACP, filed a lawsuit against the School Board asking for accelerated desegregation of students and teachers and adequate transportation to allow all children access to integrated schools. It was 1969 before the Lee County school system was finally fully desegregated–15 years after the Supreme Court had handed down its decision. Lee County was one of the last counties in the United States to fully integrate its school system.

That lawsuit filed by NAACP resulted in school choice, a solution Veronica feels brought students and the community together. "We had Fort Myers High School and Dunbar High School, which was the one school where we were able to do everything from kindergarten to 12th grade. [But] they were going to close that one down [and] they were busing all the Afro-American children all over the place." It started with Colonial Elementary, built in a gray area that had not been used before for schools, and extended to the roads and transportation necessary to make school choice a reality. "That is why we have schools in all areas now: Lehigh Acres, Cape Coral, South Fort Myers."

In recognizing Veronica Shoemaker for her accomplishments, President Barack Obama wrote:

"No force for change is more powerful than that of Americans making a difference in their communities. Across our country active citizens, like Veronica Shoemaker, have dedicated their lives and careers to opening doors of opportunity for others. Their work reminds us of our charge to empower others and to build a brighter day for our children and grandchildren."

A reformer and game changer

Veronica's activist mentality drove her next into the political arena. In 1966 she ran for Fort Myers City Council and lost. She mounted campaigns for the next 16 years, running for whatever political seat was open whether it was school board, city council, county commission, or hospital board. She could not get elected because of at-large voting–where everyone in every ward voted for all the candidates.

Linda Benson's rendering of Veronica Shoemaker, who is recognized in the national *Who's Who of Distinguished Black Americans* for her extraordinary accomplishments. (*Courtesy of the artist.*)

Ultimately, the NAACP filed a lawsuit to get single-member districts in Fort Myers. But Veronica did not wait for the court's favorable ruling to take effect. "I was elected in 1982 in the last at-large election. All five wards voted for me. Today, single-member districts are in effect for election of all city council members. That changed the whole picture of how we get elected, which I think is good."

After 17 years, winning the election was not just a milestone for Veronica. "I felt like I had opened doors for others to be elected." Among the other causes for which she advocated over the years were fair wages, voting rights and equal education. "We must never forget voter registration and education," Veronica insists. "That is the key, believe you me. Voting is a master key to the continuation and the implementation of what has happened in the last 100 years. The NAACP has been the mother, the father, the sister, the brother that has kept this civil rights movement together. But we can't sit back and take it for granted."

Harkening back to her days of growing vegetables and tending citrus and other fruit trees, Veronica also opened a florist shop in 1975, which is still family owned and operated. "That was one of the most joyous moments of my life," the mother of three once said. "I just loved the feeling of independence from owning my own building and my own business."

Many life lessons can be derived from Veronica Shoemaker's public and business life, among them the value of civic involvement, attitude and persistence. "One of the life lessons that I learned (from her example) is to never give up," said 14-year-old Canterbury School student John "JJ" Gamba, who was inspired by her life to produce a video about her that reflects in-depth research, interviews with those who know and have worked with her, and conversations he had with her.

The "firsts" just don't stop for Veronica Shoemaker. In 2010 she was awarded the first ever Hodges University Luminary Award.* In Fort Myers Veronica Shoemaker has both a boulevard and a lane named after her.

---

*The Hodges University Luminary Award "is presented to a citizen(s) who personifies society's most valued human characteristics and thus has moved society in a positive way, serving as a distinguished example of the virtues of perseverance, honesty, moral character and charity."

BERNESE "BERNE" BARFIELD DAVIS

"First Lady of Fort Myers"

In 2009, Bernese Barfield Davis was named by the Southwest Florida Museum of History Foundation as the first recipient of its History Maker of the Year Award. Former mayor Jim Humphrey promptly dubbed her the "First Lady of Fort Myers." In many ways, this outstanding woman is a product of the influence exerted by the female pioneers of yesterday. As importantly, through her philanthropy and example, their legacy will continue to impact Fort Myers' residents and visitors for generations to come.

Berne was born in 1914 in Hamilton County, Florida, just a stone's throw from the Florida-Georgia line. Her father worked in the saw mills, moving from camp to camp. When Berne was 14, the family moved to Slater, in what is now part of North Fort Myers.

"Looking back now, I think we'd be called underprivileged," says Berne of her childhood. But she was oblivious to her social-economic status at the time. She was a teenager in a new town, making friends and hitching rides to Fort Myers High School in her big brother's Model T.

The year was 1929, and Berne had barely learned the names of her teachers and classmates when the stock market crashed and the country was plunged into the Great Depression. But Fort Myers was spared the cataclysmic unemployment experienced by the great industrial cities in the northeast, partly because of a building project that started around that time on the corner of Jackson and

First Streets in downtown Fort Myers. It involved the construction of a grand limestone-and-coral clad post office designed by prominent Florida architect Nat Gaillard Walker.

There are conflicting reports about how Fort Myers got such an incredibly beautiful post office. Karl Grismer states in *The Story of Fort Myers* that the building was secured largely through the efforts of B.C. Foxworthy, who had been active for years in Republican politics. During the Hoover administration, he kept bombarding Washington with requests until Congress finally gave in and approved the necessary appropriation. But Berne Davis, among others, believes that Thomas Edison played a role. He invited President Hoover to Fort Myers in February of 1929 to help him celebrate his 82nd birthday, and after Hoover returned from Edison's birthday party at the Pleasure Palace, Congress suddenly found the money needed to build the new post office.

In the next few years, Fort Myers weathered many economic storms, including the failure of the Bank of Fort Myers in 1931, the Lee County Bank and Trust Company in 1932, and the First National Bank after that. But work on the stately neoclassical revival edifice continued. It opened for business on October 30, 1933. Berne had graduated four months earlier, and having watched the building go up throughout her teenage years, she formed an emotional attachment to the structure, which was reputed at the time to be "the most attractive post office in a city of this size in America."

Chance meetings change lives

After graduation, Berne worked as a secretary for the Chamber of Commerce

Berne and Sidney Davis. (Courtesy of Sidney & Berne Davis Art Center.)

Berne Davis' donation to help restore the former post office to the grandeur it once enjoyed will have an enduring impact on the community she loves. (Courtesy of Thomas P. Hall, 2011.)

and a local attorney and municipal bond business. On evenings and weekends, she "cruised the Main" with her girlfriends, hoping to make a date with one of the Philadelphia Athletics or an up-and-coming businessman. Berne never scored a date with a ball player, but she did meet Sidney Davis.

"Sidney was invited to a party but his regular date, Barbara Mann's sister, was not able to go," explains Berne. "A mutual friend in the Junior Chamber of Commerce introduced us. I didn't think he would want to go out with me as he was 13 years older, but he invited me to go to the party with him and our romance began.

"Sidney was one of the nicest persons I ever met. He was the most unselfish man I ever met, and he was the love of my life. I never met anyone who could come up to Sidney. He was concerned and considerate of people, and very public-spirited, as was I. So we had that in common. He thought Fort Myers was heaven on earth. What little we had, he always wanted to spend it in Fort Myers. Other people would go to Naples to buy cars. Not us. He would get furious if I went to Tampa and bought a dress."

Sidney had a nose for business. He was born and raised in the coastal community of Chincoteague, Virginia, not far from the Maryland border. His father was the lighthouse keeper and an oyster dealer, but after graduating from high school, Sidney took a job in the local bank instead of following his father into the oyster business. It was 1925, and Sidney and some of his buddies heard about the real estate boom taking place in Florida. Both a risk taker and budding entrepreneur, Sidney joined with his friends in buying some property in Tampa, "sight unseen." Then he hopped on a train to visit his investment.

Aerial view of the Sidney & Berne Davis Art Center. (Courtesy of Sidney & Berne Davis Art Center.)

On the way to Tampa, Sidney had the good fortune to meet Colonel J.W. Blanding, the president of Lee County Bank, Title & Trust Co. When the Colonel learned that Sidney worked in a bank, he invited him to Fort Myers. "You need to come to Fort Myers," he told the young man. "It's going to be something someday."

Sidney took him up on his offer and visited Fort Myers several days later. The Colonel offered him a job on the spot for a great deal more money than Sidney was making in Chincoteague. Sidney told the Colonel he would go home and think about it. "Oh no," Colonel Blanding told Sidney. "Don't do that. Just telegram them your resignation." And he did. Sidney it seems also thought that Fort Myers was going to be something someday.

While employed at the bank, Sidney met two couples who changed his life and helped shape Berne's later civic-mindedness and philanthropy. The first couple was Billie Jewett and her husband.

"The Jewetts came to Fort Myers later in 1925 after Sidney had started at Lee County Bank," Berne recalls. "They built a home in 1926 that they intended to live in three months out of the year. They wanted a live-in caretaker for the other nine months. Sidney was living in a boarding house at the time, so when they offered him the position, he jumped at it. He moved in and never moved out."

The Jewetts built one of the most elaborate Spanish Colonial structures ever erected in Fort Myers. The U-shaped two-story home still stands. Located at 1141 Wales Drive, it is referred to today as the Jewett-Thompson House, and it was added to the National Register of Historic Places in 1988.

"Billie Jewett opened doors for Sidney and made opportunities available to us we wouldn't have otherwise enjoyed," Berne says with deep appreciation. "But she knew she could depend on Sidney for everything and trust him implicitly."

Contrary to popular opinion, the post office was not a WPA project. The project was completed (October 30, 1933) and dedicated (December 9, 1933) before the Civil Works Administration (CWA), Federal Emergency Relief Administration (FERA) and Work Projects Administrations (WPA) were ever authorized. Lee County did, however, have three banner WPA projects: the Lee County Airport at present-day Page Field, the new Lee Memorial Hospital, and the waterfront park and yacht basin.

When the federal government opts to abandon a structure, it first offers the property to the host state, then the county and finally the municipality. In this case, the State of Florida and Lee County both passed on the old post office. The City of Fort Myers exercised its option and purchased the building and entire city block for $186,000, which is some $14,000 less than it cost to erect the building in 1933. The City of Fort Myers then leased the building to Florida Arts for $1/year for 99 years subject to the obligation that Florida Arts rehabilitate and restore the building to its original condition.

To reward his integrity, dependability and loyalty, Jewett loaned Sidney the money he needed to buy the Heitman Clothing Store when it became available in 1934. "Billie wouldn't take any interest from him and she sold us the tract on the river for $500 where we built our home [in 1942]."

Sidney also met Thomas and Mina Edison while he was employed at the Lee County Bank. They became fast friends. By the time Sidney and Berne started dating, Thomas Edison had passed away, but Sidney maintained his friendship with Mina. "When he told Mrs. Edison we were going to be married, she wanted to meet me," Berne recalls of their first meeting. "I was frightened to death to meet her, but she invited us for dinner and Sidney insisted we go." To a girl whose father worked in a saw mill and who had worked as a secretary since graduating from high school, Mina Edison possessed the aura of an Oprah Winfrey by today's standards.

"Sidney introduced me and she held out her arms and hugged me. My fears just melted away because she was so sweet and nice," Berne fondly recalls. "She liked flowers, gardens and clothes, and we had lots of woman talk." So began a friendship that lasted until Mina Edison's death in 1947.

Seat of women's socio-political power in '30-'40s

During the intervening 14 years, Mina Edison exposed her newfound friend to the world of garden clubs. In the 1930s and '40s, garden clubs were important social organizations that not only initiated civic beautification projects, but demonstrated for the first time in American history that women could wield positive socio-political power within their communities.

In 1938, Fort Myers began celebrating Edison and his achievements through the Edison Festival of Light. Berne was on the festival's first court, as was Sidney. The following year, she was crowned Queen. As the festival's Lord Chamberlain that year, it was Sidney who had the honor of placing the tiara on his fiancée. On July 6, 1939, the couple married. "He was a confirmed bachelor," Berne chuckles. "No one thought he would ever marry."

Like most, Sidney and Berne had no money when they started out, but because of the men's clothing store, that slowly changed. And since they were never blessed with children, Berne spent much of her time volunteering in the community. "I helped at Lee Memorial Hospital, serving on the Board. At the Red Cross, I made bandages during the war and served on their Board as well. And, of course, I belonged to the Fort Myers/Lee County Garden Council." She was also a founding member of the Altar Guild at the First United Methodist Church.

The post office took on added significance for Berne during this time. Although she never helped out in her husband's clothing store, she visited Sidney there often. Located in the front of the Arcade Building on First Street (where Arts for ACT Gallery is located today), the shop was just half a block from the post office, and Berne quite naturally associated one with the other.

Over the decades that followed, Sidney and Berne immersed themselves in numerous civic organizations and projects. He was a president and director of the Chamber of Commerce, president of the Merchants Association and Kiwanis Club, a director of Lee Memorial Hospital, and a member of the Masonic Lodge, Shrine, Fort Myers Country Club, Executive Club and Junior Chamber of Commerce. He was active in their church. Tremendously interested in education, Sidney helped many kids go to college. And the Sidney Davis Men's Store was the pinnacle of male fashion and haberdashery until the mid-1960s, when downtown Fort Myers lost most of its foot traffic and shops following the opening of the Edison Mall. But Sidney invested wisely, and by the time he died in 1989 (just a few months shy of their 50th wedding anniversary), he had built a sizeable nest egg, leaving Berne a comfortably wealthy widow.

After Sidney's passing, Berne continued to cultivate the vision of the community that she and Sidney had shared for the preceding half century, but her subsequent activities and interests were clearly influenced by the lessons she learned from her mentors, Mina Edison and Billie Jewett.

A healing and generous presence

Inspired by Mina's example, Berne restored Mina's moonlight garden at the Edison & Ford Winter Estates and helped establish the garden at the Fort Myers/Lee County Garden Council around the corner on Virginia Street. She served on the boards of Edison State College (now Florida SouthWestern State College), the Edison College Foundation, and the Clinic for the Rehabilitation of Wildlife on Sanibel Island. She was involved for years in the Edison Festival of Light, and as the first president of the Fort Myers Women's Golf Association, she initiated sweeping landscape improvements to the Fort Myers Country Club. And combining the love she and Mina Edison shared for horticulture with Sidney's commitment to education and research, she gave $620,159 to Florida Gulf Coast University in 2006 to create an endowed chair for horticultural education. It is called the Bernese B. and Sidney R. Davis Chair for Landscape Design, Horticultural Education and Research. Berne's generous gift spurred a matching contribution of $434,411 from the State of Florida Major Gifts Trust Fund, bringing the total endowment to nearly $1.1 million.

Inspired by the memory of Billie Jewett establishing a wing at Lee Memorial Hospital, Berne established a healing garden for patients of the new Regional Cancer Center in 2008. Berne understands the pain and heartache experienced by cancer patients and their families. She lost Sidney, her brother and a host of friends and acquaintances to the disease. "If I can give a patient or saddened family member five minutes of joy in the new healing garden," says Berne, "then my work is done."

"We were deeply touched when Berne decided to bring her passion in life to the cancer patients of Lee Memorial Health System," stated the hospital when the gift was first announced. "Her gift of a healing garden to the new Lee Cancer Center is truly a gift from the heart. Berne knows the joy of a new bloom, wandering pathway or visiting butterfly and wants to share that gift with those members of our community who are suffering from this devastating disease. The healing garden will contain pathways for reflection, a number of aromatic herbs and plants, relaxing water fountains, and quiet spaces for staff and patients to talk, share and heal."

Though the healing garden is Berne's most visible gift to the hospital, she has also served as a past Board member, co-founded the Pink Ladies Volunteer Group, served on the Hospital Auxiliary, and given her time and energy in countless other ways.

But it may be her donation to help restore the former post office to the grandeur it once enjoyed that may have the greatest and most enduring impact on the community she loves.

Gifts that keep on giving

Around the same time the downtown business district began losing shops and stores to the new mall in the 1960s, the federal government built a new post office on Monroe and converted the old post office building into a federal courthouse. To conceal the ductwork for the central heating and cooling system that was added at that time (circa 1966-67), holes were cut in walls and drop ceilings were installed that covered up many of the beautiful architectural features that Nat Walker had included in the building's original design. When the federal judiciary also moved to new quarters in 1998, the federal employees in charge of the property inexplicably made no effort to protect the building's interior. They simply turned off the power and locked the doors, subjecting the delicate wood moldings and granite floors to damage from mold, mildew and ravages of a leaky roof.

One day after the city purchased the site and leased the old building to Jim Griffith and Florida Arts, Berne and friends Barbara Mann* and Caroline Hill decided to have a look at the damage for themselves. The threesome had been enjoying lunch at a nearby eatery and, in spite of Berne and Barbara being in their nineties, the trio crawled through the debris strewn across the rear entry in order to satisfy their curiosity. "Jim Griffith was there, working," Berne recounts of the episode. "I thought the floor was dirt, but Jim said, no, it's just all the mold and mud that was stopping us from seeing the original granite floors."

The encounter no doubt planted a seed in Berne's mind. Something needed to be done to save the old landmark. But it took a surprise drive-by for Berne to decide that she needed to kick off the drive to raise the $6 million needed for restoration and rehabilitation of the old building.

"My sister Eunice picked me up one night and drove me over to the post office. I saw all these colors on the columns and walls, and I asked Eunice if they'd painted the building. But they hadn't. It was the lights from the bronze sculptures they put in on the sidewalk outside the building. It was so beautiful I made the decision right then and there to donate the money."

And so Berne donated $1 million to Florida Arts and her and Sidney's names were chiseled into the limestone above the building's slender Ionic columns and broad steps.

"Having no children, Sidney thought I should do something constructive," says Berne, giving rare insight into the mind of a philanthropist. "The Art Center is constructive. What Jim Griffith is doing down there is constructive. It's wonderful having a building capable of doing all the things he has planned."

By virtue of the venue it provides and the art exhibitions, concerts and performances, events, classes and workshops, and community outreach it conducts, the Sidney & Berne Davis Art Center will positively influence generations of new visual and performing artists, filmmakers and

The bronze sculptures that Eunice took Berne to see the night she decided to donate $1 million toward the post office's restoration is called Caloosahatchee Manuscripts. It was created by internationally acclaimed light sculptor Jim Sanborn in 2001 for Florida Power & Light Co., which donated the public artwork to the City of Fort Myers to commemorate the conversion of its power plant from oil to natural gas. The city had Sanborn install the drums outside the Art Center, which cast an alphabet soup of lighted letters on the façade of the building after dark each night.

---

*Berne Davis and Barbara Mann were friends for more than 80 years. Berne first met Barbara at Fort Myers High School, when she was a student and Barbara worked as a secretary for the principal. The two lived a couple of doors away from each other on the river for many years.

educators. Many will remain in the community. Some will extend the reach of the Art Center and, derivatively Berne's gift, to other parts of the country, if not the world. The Center has also breathed new life and vitality into the downtown historic district by making it a cultural destination not only for locals and out-of-town visitors, but for internationally acclaimed artists and world-renowned musicians, dancers and other performers.

"Sidney believed in preserving the best of the past for the future," notes Berne. "That is why I wanted to have his name on the old post office."

As Bernese Barfield Davis' story so aptly illustrates, the lessons taught by our mentors are not confined to the past. They can impact the culture and quality of life in a community for generations to come.

HELEN JOHNSON HENDRY

Pioneer and Trailblazer in Florida's Landscape Industry

Fate played a role when, at the age of six, Helen Elizabeth Johnson and her family moved from Georgia to a house located behind the first nursery in South Florida, the 40-acre Everglades Nursery on McGregor. In 1942 at age 12, Helen landed an after-school job at the nursery pulling weeds to earn money to buy Christmas presents for her parents and six siblings. With that job Helen discovered her love for plants, and after graduating from Fort Myers High School, she accelerated to full-time employment at the nursery, setting the stage for a trailblazing career in horticulture and landscape architecture.

From its inception in 1909, the Everglades Nursery specialized in semitropical plants, trees and shrubs, particularly the bougainvillea, and became a frequent source of plants for the Edison estate. The nursery's founder, James E. Hendry, Jr., was the grandson of Southwest Florida pioneer and city father, Captain F.A. Hendry, who claimed the first bougainvillea in Florida, a gift from a sea captain who was visiting the area. Under James Jr.'s direction, Everglades Nursery would play a key role in cultivating and popularizing the plant both regionally and nationally, and Helen would assist in that achievement.

Helen got the chance to prove her talent right away. In 1947 Mina Edison deeded the 13-acre Edison Estate to the City of

Fort Myers* to perpetuate her husband's memory and legacy. Helen was already intimately familiar with the grounds. She had often wandered around the gardens, sometimes consulting with Mina on landscaping matters even though she was just a teenager. Now the budding landscape architect had room to spread her wings. She helped design landscaping installations at the Estate that included the traffic-stopping, rosy-pink bougainvillea hedge along the north boundary. Planted in the 1950s, it is one of the most famous landmarks in Fort Myers and many consider it to be among Helen's finest designs. In fact, she played such a critical role in the beautification of the nonprofit property and throughout the region as a "tree pioneer" that Estates President/CEO Chris Pendleton endearingly says Helen "built her career from the ground up."

During the 1950s and '60s Everglades Nursery was a forerunner in supplying flowering trees and specimen palms to theme parks including Cypress Gardens, Walt Disney World and the 1964 New York World's Fair. In the '50s, it was the original nursery to sell hurricane-blown palms to theme parks for their dramatic, curved trunks. Over the years, James Jr. and Helen introduced successful pollination and grafting methods that changed the color palette of plants in South Florida, particularly working with gardenia, bougainvillea, and hibiscus. It is no wonder that the nursery became one of the largest of its kind in the world, shipping plants to Arizona, California, Texas, and Canada.

"The young Helen and her employer and mentor shared a deep sense of mutual admiration," wrote the *Fort Myers News-Press* following an interview in

---

By 1988, the adjacent Henry Ford winter estate had been purchased, and the Edison & Ford Winter Estates now totaled 20 acres. It is one of the most visited historic home sites in the country.

Helen Elizabeth Johnson pictured here at graduation from Fort Myers High School. (Courtesy of *The News-Press* Archives.)

Helen Johnson Hendry was the first female certified by the State of Florida's Board of Landscape Architects. (Courtesy of *The News-Press* Archives.)

2014. "He hybridized and named a thornless bougainvillea variety for her; she propagated and named a yellow hibiscus for him." Helen credits her mentor, nursery owner and future father-in-law with teaching her everything she knew.

After the death of James Jr. in 1955, Helen continued her innovative work at the nursery and in 1969 she married her mentor's son, James E. Hendry III. They managed the nursery, along with Helen's brother Frank until 1984, when James III died. The nursery property was sold in 1987 to a land developer and, no longer managing the nursery, Helen was free to start practicing the art of landscape architecture.

She worked with many prominent clients in Naples, Fort Myers, Sanibel and Captiva Island. She left an indelible mark as far south as Key West through her expert efforts in beautifying private residences, commercial developments, and municipal and government projects. As a result, she was honored by numerous organizations, including the Florida Federation of Garden Councils, Florida Nursery Growers Palm Chapter, and the PACE Center for Girls of Lee County, which designated her one of their Grand Dames in 2010.

She became a director of the Florida Nursery, Growers and Landscape Association (FNGLA), where she lobbied the Florida State Legislature for passage of a bill requiring registration and examination of landscape architects. She was inducted into FNGLA's 2010 Hall of Fame, a lifetime achievement award given to a person "who has given unselfishly of their time and effort having contributed to the industry through pioneering, teaching, production, legislation, marketing, services or research."

She served on the Board of Landscape Architects for 14 years and was the third person and first female certified by the State of Florida's Board of

James E. Hendry Jr., considered one of Florida's leading horticulturists, became one of Fort Myers' first Park Commissioners and helped secure a $1,000 appropriation for city beautification projects. Later Hendry procured a city contract to plant 6,000 trees throughout Fort Myers. This was one of the largest beautification projects Fort Myers would ever initiate. Hendry suggested to city officials that Fort Myers be nicknamed "City of Palms" and the city has been known as that ever since. (Courtesy of Southwest Florida Historical Society.)

Landscape Architects. Her permit simply bears the numerals "03" in the space where the license number is printed. Helen is currently a Trustee of the Edison & Ford Winter Estates and honors the legacy of Thomas and Mina Edison with her continued service as a consultant for the County Roadside Beautification Committee.

AFTERWORD

Each of the women you've just read about left their imprint on the story of Fort Myers. For some, their legacy, while amorphous, is profound. Had Christiana Vivas not decided to stay and had Jane L. Hendry not decided to come to the land encompassed by the old frontier fort, it is likely that the town would have been settled years later in some other place, under some other name and without the involvement of inventor Thomas Edison, hotelier Paul O'Neill or steel magnate Ambrose McGregor.

Others, like Tootie McGregor Terry, impacted the town's infrastructure, amenities and topography. It was Tootie, after all, who convinced the downtown business owners to extend the waterfront 200 feet into the Caloosahatchee and build a seawall from Monroe Street all the way to Billy's Creek. Ella Mae Piper not only gave the town nickel soft drinks and its first beauty parlor, she made it possible for black youngsters from hundreds of miles around to not only get a high school education for the very first time, but also get into college. At the same time, Melissa Jones and Candis Walker made it possible for people of color to receive treatment and health care in a hospital. Their influence would have undoubtedly been even greater had it not been for the limiting effect of segregation and the Jim Crow laws in force during their day.

Flossie Hill, Olive Stout, Julia Allen Hanson and Mina Edison demonstrated that women could assume leadership roles in the arts, culture, civic beautification and business long before women obtained the right to vote and hold political office. This they did by organizing women's clubs, garden clubs, reading rooms and the town's first library and forming coalitions outside their own organizations in order to implement their progressive vision for the town's future.

Helen Johnson Hendry played a pivotal role in propagating and popularizing the use of the vibrantly colorful bougainvillea that adorn homes and offices throughout Southwest Florida today, while a number of others improved quality of life for every resident and visitor through the contributions they made to the arts, culture and education. Four women in particular continue to exert their influence on current and future generations through the institutions they created during their lives. Mina Edison, Ella Mae Piper, Barbara Mann and Berne Davis occupy this pantheon of exceptional women.

In 1947, a prescient Mina Edison deeded Seminole Lodge and the rest of the Edisons' winter estate to the City of Fort Myers in order to perpetuate her husband's name and fame. Today, the Edison & Ford Winter Estates treats more than 250,000 people each year to informative tours of its 20 acres of historical buildings, historic gardens, the Edison Botanic Research Lab and the Edison Ford Museum, instilling in them a deeper appreciation for the genius and accomplishments of both Thomas Edison and his friend and winter neighbor, Henry Ford. Under the innovative stewardship of President Chris Pendleton, the Edison & Ford Winter Estates inspires new generations of inventors, business owners, horticulturalists, history buffs and artists through a series of ambitious science, history and arts classes, workshops and summer camps, as well as compelling exhibitions in its historic Caretaker's Cottage. In so doing, the Edison & Ford Winter Estates extends the dynamic legacy of Mina Edison for generations to come.

Nearly a decade later, Ella Mae Piper followed her friend and mentor's example by donating her home to the City of Fort Myers "for the benefit of young people and the elderly." The new Dr. Ella Mae Piper Center for Social Services carries on her work today by enhancing the social and economic well-being of Southwest Florida residents 55 and older and by making a positive impact in the lives of frail elderly, at-risk youths, special-needs children, and the community at large.

It may be impossible to quantify the impact Barbara Mann and Berne Davis have and continue to make in attracting, educating and inspiring new waves of visual artists, filmmakers, musicians, dancers, thespians and other performing artists who have the opportunity to take center stage at the Barbara Mann Performing Arts Hall and Sidney & Berne Davis Art Center. Additionally, having been inspired by friend and mentor Mina Edison's civic leadership, love of landscaping and involvement in garden clubs, Berne endowed a chair at Florida Gulf Coast University for landscape design and horticultural education and research that will produce landscape architects, designers and horticulturalists for decades to come.

Today, a new generation of female leaders is impacting our lives by creating legacies in the arts, business, education, healthcare and the ecology of Southwest Florida. Local NPR affiliate WGCU calls them "makers" and has been formally recognizing their contributions since 2013. We applaud this initiative and hope that the examples set by Fort Myers' nearly forgotten early female pioneers further inspires this and future generations of makers, whether they live and work here in Southwest Florida or someplace else in our global community.

References

Albion, Michele Wehrwein. (2010, October). Irrepressible Ella. *Gulfshore Life*. Retrieved from http://www.gulfshorelife.com/.

Chestnut, Cathy. (2014, April 20). *Tropicalia: Learn about a local legend. News-Press*, Retrieved from http://www.news-press.com.

Davis, Berne. Personal interview by Thomas P. Hall. 25 March 2011.

Ershowski, Phyllis. (2007, July 12). Profiles: Veronica Shoemaker: A life in full bloom. *Florida Weekly*. Retrieved from fortmyers.floridaweekly.com.

First United Methodist Church. (2010, April 11). First Church Connections, Issue 15.

Gamba, John (Producer). (2012). *Veronica Shoemaker: A Symbol of Defiance and Determination in Fort Myers* [video]. Available from https://vimeo.com/45078154.

Gannon, Michael. *Florida: A Short History*, University Press of Florida, 2003.

Godown, Marian and Alberta Rawchuck. *Yesterday's Fort Myers*. Fort Myers: Press Printing, 1975.

Grismer, Karl H. *The Story of Fort Myers: The History of the Land of the Caloosahatchee and Southwest Florida*, Southwest Florida Historical Society, Island Press, 1982.

Grismer, Karl H. and D.B. McKay, Ed. *Tampa: A History of the City of Tampa and the Tampa Bay Region of Florida*. St. Petersburg Printing Company, Inc., 1950.

Jacobs, T.M. *H.E. Heitman, An Early Entrepreneur of Fort Myers*. 2009.

LeGrand, Mark (Producer). (2010). *Hall of Fame Inductees* [video]. Available from http://www.fngla.org/.

Miguel-Navarro, Tracy and Katy Torralbas. (2009, Feb 11). A Lifetime of Changes: Reflecting on the NAACP's 100-year anniversary. *Naples Daily News* online edition. http://www.naplesnews.com/.

New York Times. 1902, September 9. Obituary of Bradford McGregor. Retrieved from http://www.nytimes.com/.

Reaves, Gerri. *Legendary Locals of Fort Myers*, Charleston, SC: Arcadia Publishing, 2012.

Turner, Gregg. *Fort Myers in Vintage Postcards*. Charleston, SC: Arcadia Publishing, 2005. Print.

Turner, Gregg and Stan Mulford. *Images of America: Fort Myers*. Charleston, SC: Arcadia Publishing, 2001. Print.

Venable, John D. *Mina Miller Edison: Daughter, Wife and Mother of Inventors*. Charles Edison Fund, Newark, New Jersey, 1981. Retrieved from http://www.edisonmuckers.org/daughter-wife-and-mother-of-inventors/.

Weatherford, Doris. *They Dared to Dream: Florida Women Who Shaped History*. Gainesville: University Press of Florida, 2015.

Wickham, Gertrude. 1914. *Pioneer Families of Cleveland*, Evangelical Publishing House, 1914.

Wilson, Milton. *Pioneer Families of Polk County and South Florida, the Wilson family: with data on the Alderman family, the Carleton family, the Hendry family, the McFail family, the Hurst family, the Knight family, the Varn family (and allied families)*. Place of publication and publisher not identified.

INDEX

ABOUT THE AUTHORS

Robin C. Tuthill has been a writer and editor since 1980, working primarily in newspaper and magazine feature writing, medical writing/editing, and academic writing/editing. Five years after completing a 7-day "Life and Career Renewal" Outward Bound in her late 30s, Robin earned a master's degree in religious studies at the University of South Florida. She taught classes in comparative religion; created the inaugural issue of *The Journal of the Society for the Study of Metaphysical Religion* (JSSMR), an international, academic journal; and authored four editions of the *Instructor's Manual and Test Questions* that accompanied *World Religions Today*, a college textbook published by Oxford University Press.

Robin facilitated "Freeing the Writer Within" classes and ongoing writing groups from 1995-2015. In the creative writing workshop that she developed, she witnessed over and over again the strength and confidence that come from self-discovery as participants wrote and shared their stories. She believes that the power of the written word to achieve self-transformation cannot be over-estimated. She holds a bachelor's degree in English from Purdue University, and masters' degrees in education and religious studies from the University of South Florida.

She was born and raised in St. Petersburg, Florida into a family that spent weekends boating and fishing the waters of Tampa Bay and the Gulf of Mexico. Robin lives in North Fort Myers, where she continues to write and enjoy Florida's natural beauty.

Thomas P. Hall is an art journalist, arts advocate and local historian. Since January of 2011, Tom has published more than 5,000 art-related articles for Examiner.com, Art Southwest Florida, *Gulf Coast Times, Art District Magazine, River Weekly News* and Toti Media, publisher of *Gulf & Main, Bonita & Estero* and *RSW Living* magazines.

As founder and editor of Art Southwest Florida, a free one-stop art destination website, Tom has profiled the more than sixty outdoor art fairs and festivals that take place from Marco to Matlacha Island each season, most of the leading art galleries and centers that collectively make Southwest Florida the number one small art market in the country, and the public art collections of Florida Gulf Coast University, Lee County and the cities of Fort Myers, Naples and Bonita Springs. It was while researching the dozens of sculptures, murals and other artworks that dot Southwest Florida that Tom discovered that each piece uniquely expresses the history and heritage of the communities in which they are located. Today, Tom shares those and many other stories with his readers through his "on this day in local history" posts on Art Southwest Florida.

In recognition of his numerous contributions to the arts and culture of the region, Tom was nominated for a Lee County Visitor & Convention Bureau and Greater Fort Myers Chamber of Commerce 2013 Celebration of Business and Tourism Chrysalis Award for Cultural Achievement.

Born and raised in northern New Jersey, Tom has made Florida his home for more than 45 years. He holds bachelors, masters and juris doctorate degrees from the University of Florida.